# OBJECT RELATIONS THEORY

# OBJECT RELATIONS THEORY

RICHARD J. KOSCIEJEW

authorHOUSE®

AuthorHouse™
1663 Liberty Drive
Bloomington, IN 47403
www.authorhouse.com
Phone: 1-800-839-8640

© 2013 by Richard J. Kosciejew. All rights reserved.

No part of this book may be reproduced, stored in a retrieval system, or transmitted by any means without the written permission of the author.

Published by AuthorHouse    04/27/2013

ISBN: 978-1-4817-1333-7 (sc)
ISBN: 978-1-4817-1334-4 (e)

Library of Congress Control Number: 2013902356

Any people depicted in stock imagery provided by Thinkstock are models, and such images are being used for illustrative purposes only.
Certain stock imagery © Thinkstock.

This book is printed on acid-free paper.

Because of the dynamic nature of the Internet, any web addresses or links contained in this book may have changed since publication and may no longer be valid. The views expressed in this work are solely those of the author and do not necessarily reflect the views of the publisher, and the publisher hereby disclaims any responsibility for them.

# CONTENTS

An Introduction..................................................................................vii

Chapter One
Instinct Versus Relationships............................................................ 1

Chapter Two
The Psychogenesis of Manic-Depressive States............................ 6

Chapter Three
Object Concept and Object Choice ............................................27

Chapter Four
Object Relationships and Affects..................................................45

Chapter Five
Narcissistic Object Choice in Women .......................................65

Chapter Six
Structural Derivatives of Object Relationships ........................82

Chapter Seven
The Therapeutic Action of Psychoanalysis.................................119

# AN INTRODUCTION

Object Relations, in psychoanalysis are those in which the emotional relations between subject and object, in that which through a process of identification, is believed to constitute the developing ego. In this context, the word object refers to any person or thing, or representational aspect of them, with which the subject forms an intense emotional relationship.

Object relations were first described by German psychoanalyst Karl Abraham in an influential paper, published in 1924. In the paper he developed the ideas of the founder of psychoanalysis, Sigmund Freud, on infantile sexuality and the development of the libido. Object-relations theory has become one of the central themes of post-Freudian psychoanalysis, particularly through the writings of British psychoanalysts Melanie Klein, Ronald Fairbairn, and Donald Winnicott, all deeply influenced by Abraham. They have each developed distinctly, though complementary, approaches to analysis, evolving theories of personal development based on early parental attachments.

Many different authors have represented and, as quickly become apparent from reading them, they often hold radically different viewpoints concerning the importance, meaning and function of 'object' and, by extension, the environment in the psychological development and mental life of individuals. Questions of the relationships between what is 'internal' and what is 'external' abound in writings on this subject. How do our significant early relationships with others become internalized and affect our subsequent view of the world and other people? What aspects of our early relationships determine those whom we choose as lover, spouse, or friend?

What is the dynamic nature of our internal object world, how does it progress as a principle of evolutionary descendability, and what are the implications of therapy? What is biologically innate in the psychology of the individual and direct environmental experience has modulated? What is the nature of motivation—the pressure of instinctual wishes or the seeking of relationships with others? Questions so unimportant that are central to an understanding of human psychology do not easily lend themselves to a unitary theory, and it may be more accurate to speak of a continuum of object relations theories.

We can discern two opposing poles of this continuum. The first lies within the classical psychoanalytic realm and sees objects as the person or thing onto which we have concentrated the biological drives. A crucial element of this view of the object is that we have cathected the mental representation of the thing or person with aggressive or libidinal energy and not the external thing or person. Arlow (1980) summarized this conceptualization: 'Fundamentally, it is the effect of unconscious fantasy wishes, connected with specific mental representations of objects that colours, distorts and affects the ultimate quality of interpersonal relations. Distinguishing it between the person and the object is important. This is essentially the core of transference, in which the person in the real world is confused with a mental representation of the childhood object, a mental representation of what was either a person or a thing.' Arlow thus emphasized the concept of the object as an intrapsychic mental representation whose evolution cannot be separated from the vicissitudes of the drives. He stated 'in later experience these (drives) become organized as for persistent unconscious fantasies that ultimately affects object choice and patterns of loving.' He further comments that it is not simply 'the experience with the object, but what is done with the experience, that is decisive for development.'

The work of W. R. Fairbairn is the opposite to Arlow's. Concepts of drives as central to human motivation are abandoned. In their place object relations are seen for being the determining factors of development. The role of the object as merely the goal of the drive to enable its discharge is replaced by the predominance of the object. Fairbairn (1952) states: 'Psychology is a study of the relationships of the individual to his objects, while, in similar terms, psychopathology may be said to resolve itself more specifically into a study of the relationship of the ego to its internalized objects.' Accountably, the experience of the object in reality becomes very important and determines psychic structure and the internal objects are viewed as reflections of experiences with real persons. Object seeking is dominant, while the pleasure principle is not. Guntrip (1961) a follower of Fairbairn writes: 'Freud's impersonal 'pleasure principle' treated the object as a mere aggregate to the end of a purely subjective and impersonal tension relieving 'process' and not sought for its intrinsic value in a relationship . . . From this point of view Fairbairn subordinates the pleasure principle to the reality-principle, which is now seen to be the object-relationships principle, wherein, Freud regards the reality-principle simply as a delayed pleasure-principle.'

Between the theories of Arlow and Fairbairn which lays range of view concerning the function of objects. Direct observation of young children and their mothers by Margaret Mahler and her colleagues has resulted in a body of 'objective' behavioural data upon which a developmental model of the infant's psychological separation from the mother has been built, a model that has major implications for object relations theory and for therapy, since some clinicians now emphasize preoedipal mother-child dyadic issues in their work with patients and trace transference back to early mother-infant interactions. Inherent in Mahler's work is a theory of the psychological development of the 'self,' the obverse side of object relations, since the intrapsychic world of the individual contains both self and object representations. The development of the self is the centre of Kohut's work that is the subject of considerable controversy among contemporary psychoanalysts.

At first sight the descriptive term 'object' seems infelicitous with its apparently dehumanizing connotation, but Freud's original use of the word was technically specific and free from mechanistic implications. He stated in the first of his 'Three Essays on the Theory of Sexuality' (1905): 'I will at this point introduce two technical terms. Let us call the person from whom sexual attraction proceeds the sexual object and the act toward which the instinct tends the sexual aim. Scientifically sifting observations, then, shows that numerous deviations occur in respect of both—the sexual object and the sexual aim.' Thus, the sexual object is tied directly to the instinct, the sexual drive, and is subservient to it. In the third of these essays, Freud stated: 'This ego-libido is, however, only conveniently accessible to analytic study when it has been put to the use of cathecting sexual objects, that is, when it has become object-libido. We can then perceive it concentrating upon objects, becoming fixed upon them or abandoning them, moving from one object to another and, from these situations, directing the subject's sexual activity, which leads to the satisfaction, that is to the partial and temporary extinction of the libido.' It should be noted that Freud is here referring to mental representations of objects, and not objects in the external world.

In his paper 'On Narcissism' Freud (1914) postulated that there is an original libidinal cathexis of the ego (the term 'ego' refers to the self and does not have the specialized meaning that it acquires in the later (1923) structural theory of id, ego, and superego). Part of this cathexis is later in developments given off to objects, but this object libido remains connected to an ego libido 'much as the body of an amoeba is related to the pseudopodia out which is put.' Freud asks the question about what makes it necessary for one to pass beyond the limits of narcissism (an ego libido) and to attach libidos to objects. His answer is found in the economic model: 'When the cathexis of the ego with the libido exceeds a certain amount . . . our mental apparatus for being primarily a device designed for mastering excitation that would otherwise be felt as distressing or would have pathogenic effects,' In his 1915 paper 'Instincts and their Vicissitudes' Freud stated: 'When the purely narcissistic stage has given place to the object-stage, pleasure and unpleasure signify relations of the ego to the object. If the object becomes a source of pleasurable feelings, a motor urge is set up which seeks to bring the object closer to the ego and to incorporate it into the ego.' Here the concept of internalization of objects is introduced.

In 'Mourning and Melancholia' (1917) Freud postulated a mechanism of internalization: 'The ego wants to incorporate the object into itself and according to the oral or cannibalistic phase of libidinal development . . . it wants to do so by devouring it.' In 'Group Psychology and the Analysis of the Ego' (1921) Freud viewed identification as the earliest expression of an emotional tie with another person and sees it as ambivalent from the beginning: 'It behaves like a derivative of the first oral phase of the organization of the libido in which the object that we long for and prize is assimilated by eating and is in that way annihilates as such. The cannibal, as we know, has remained at this standpoint, he has a devouring affection for his enemies and only devours people of whom he is fond.' If an object is lost in the individual, identification occurs with the lost object as a substitute for it and is introjected into the ego.

In 1923, in one of his theoretical papers, 'The Ego and the Id,' Freud posits his structural theory of psychic organization, a new conception that was profoundly to influence later psychoanalytic thinking. In this paper he stated that 'the character of the ego is a precipitate of abandoned object-cathexis and that it contains the history of these object-choices. The demolition of the oedipus complex with its giving up of his mother or an intensification of his identification with his father. 'Part of the external world has, at least, partially, been abandoned as an object and has instead by identification been taken into the ego and therefore, becomes an integral part of the internal world. This new psychical agency continues to carry the functions processed by the people (the abandoned objects) in the external world,' Therefore, occurs the formation of the superego.

It can be seen that Freud has a developed object relations theory within his work, but one that is firmly based on the primacy of the drives and of the object's being an intrapsychic mental representation cathected within sexual and aggressive energy.

In one of his last papers Freud (1940) made an eloquent and moving statement concerning the child's relationship to his fist object: 'A child's first erotic object is the mother's breast that nourishes it; love has its origin in attachment to the satisfied need for nourishment. There is no doubt that, to begin with, the child does not distinguish between the breast and its own body; when the breast has to be separated from the body and shifted to the 'outside' because the child so often finds it absent, it carries with it as an 'object' part of the original narcissistic libidinal cathexis. This first object is later completed into the person of the child's mother, who not only nourishes it, but also looks after it and thus arouses in it several of other physical sensations, pleasurable and unpleasurable. By her care of the child's body she becomes its first seducer. In these two relations lies the root of a mother's importance, unique, without parallel, established unalterably for a whole lifetime as the first and strongest lover-object and as the prototype of all later love-relations—for both sexes.'

The next major development in object relations theory after Freud is to be found in the work of Melanie Klein, the progenitor of the so-called 'British' school of object relations. Through her clinical experience with children and patients suffering from severe psychiatric illness in the 1930s and 1940s she developed an influential 'internal objects' theory. Her conception of development and psychopathology provided a springboard for Fairbairn and Winnicott's elaborations, and some of her concepts have been incorporated into the work of contemporary theorists such ss Kernberg.

Klein (1935) posits a developmental theory in which the psychological growth of the infant is governed by mechanisms of introjection and projection: 'From the beginning the ego introjects objects 'good' and 'bad' for both of which its mother's breast is the prototype—for good objects when the child obtains it and for bad when it fails him. But it is because the baby projects its own aggression onto these objects that it feels them to be 'bad' and not only in that they frustrate its desires: the child conceives of them as actually dangerous—persecutors whose fears will devour it, scoop out the inside its body, cut it to pieces, poison it—in short compassing its destruction by all the means which sadism can devise. These images, which are a fantastically distorted picture of the real objects upon which they are based, are installed by it not only in the outside world but, by the process of incorporation, also within the ego. Hence, quite little children pass through anxiety-situations (and react to them with defence mechanisms), the content of which is comparable to that of the psychoses of adults. It can be seen from this quotation that central to Klein's object relation theory is a view of the drives as motivational, but unlike Freud who developed a bipartite theory of the drives as embodying both libido and aggression, Klein gives the predominance to the aggressive drive.

In Klein's theory the role of unconscious fantasy in the mental life of the individual is also considerably extended. She sees unconscious fantasy as operating from the beginning of life, accompanying and expressing the drives. Since there are no 'objective' means of determining whether or not the newborn infant is experiencing organized fantasies (which imply the presence of a high degree of ego structure early in life) this aspect of her theory has received much less than universal acceptance.

Hanna Segal, (1964) in her monograph summarizing Klein's theories, states: 'For example, an infant going to sleep, contentedly making sucking noises and movements with his mouth or sucking his own fingers, fantasies that he is actually sucking or incorporating the breast as he goes to sleep with a fantasy of having the milk-giving breast actually inside himself. Similarly, a hungry, raging infant, screaming and kicking, fantasies that he is actually attacking the breast, tearing and destroying it, and experiences his own scream that tears him and hurts him as the torn breast is attacking him is in fact, his own insides, therefore not only does he experience of a 'wanting,' his hunger pain and his own screams may be felt as a prosecutory attack on his inside. Fantasy, but forming is a function of the ego. The views of fantasy as a mental expression of instincts through the medium of the ego assume a higher degree of ego organization than is usually postulated by Freud. It assumes that the ego from birth is capable of forming, is driven by instincts and anxiety to form primitive object relationships in fantasy and of reality. From the moment of birth the infant has to deal with the impact of reality, starting with the experience of birth itself and proceeding to endless experiences of gratification and frustration of his desires. The reality experiences immediately influenced by unconscious fantasy. Fantasy is not merely an escape from reality, but a constant and unavoidable accompaniments of real experiences, constantly interacting with them.' Segal thus notes that while unconscious fantasizing is constantly affecting perception of reality, reality does influence unconscious fantasizing. Nonetheless, there is a somewhat hermetic aspect to Klein's view of the internal mental world. (For example, Segal states: 'The importance of the environmental factor can only be correctly evaluated in relation to what it means in terms of the infant's own instincts and fantasies . . . It is when the infant has been under the sway of angry fantasies, attacking the breast, that an actual bad experience becomes much more important, since it confirms, not only his feeling that the internal world is bad, but also the sense of his own badness and the omnipotence of his malevolent fantasies'.) In some sense's Klein's is the ultimate depth psychology wherein the internal mental world has an inexorable development, and experiences of object relations in real life, and hence the environment, is of secondary importance.

Of major importance in Klein's theory is the mechanism of splitting whereby the primary object, the breast, is split into the ideal breast and persecutor breast, both of which are introjected in the internal object world. With later development in the inner world of the individual is organized around complementary fantasies of internal good and bad objects. The sense of self as good or bad is related to the relative predominance of good or bad objects in the internal world. The concept of splitting an external object into internal good and bad objects during development and later failures in integration of these two opposites in some individuals thereby preventing them experiencing both goodness and badness in the same object and thus alternating between absolute extremes of perceiving others and the self as 'all good' or 'all bad' is central to Kernberg's hypophysis of the aetiology of borderline personality disorders.

Aside from the dubious proposition that the very young infant sees elaborate mental capacities, Klein's theory of the internal object world has been criticized for its anthropomorphism and its Hieronymous Bosch-like quality of persecutor and loving internal objects, but as Guntrip (1969) observes, she developed a new conception of endopsychic structure: 'Before Klein the human psyche was regarded as an apparatus for experiencing and controlling biological instincts originating outside the ego . . . After Klein it became possible to see the human psyche as an internal world of a fully personal nature, a world of internalized ego-object relationships, which partly realistically and partly in highly distorted ways, reproduce the ego's relationships to personal objects in the real world.' Even though her theory is thorough tied to a belief in the importance of the drives she sets the stage for Fairbairn's replacement of instinct theory by a primary object relations theory.

Fairbairn, taking as his starting point Melanie Klein's conception of internalized objects, rejected Freud's instinct theory and put in its place object relationships: 'The object, and not gratification, is the ultimate aim of libidinal striving.' For Fairbairn (1954) 'the pristine personality of the child consists of a unitary dynamic ego' and 'the first defence adopted by the original ego to deal with an unsatisfying personal relationship is mental internalization, or introjection of the unsatisfying object.' Hence, the child begins with a structural ego complete withy defences that are object-related. The nature of this process of internalization, however, remains murky in Fairbairn's writing (as it does in psychoanalytic theory overall).

It was through his studies of the psychopathology of schizoid states that Fairbairn abandoned instinct theory. The schizoid individual in his view is frustrated by the acute anxiety engendered by the need to love. For the schizoid person it is love that seems to destroy, leading such individuals to withdraw from objects in the outside world for fear of destroying them. Guntrip (1961) summaries this in the following manner: 'Love-object relationships are the whole of the problem, and the conflict over them are an intense and devastating drama of need, fear, anger, and hopelessness. To attempt to account for this by a hedonistic theory of motivation, namely that the person is seeking the satisfactions of oral, anal and genital pleasure, is so impersonal and inadequate that it takes on the aspect of being itself a product of schizoid thinking. To try to reduce such problems to a quest for the pleasure of physical and emotional relaxing of sexual needs is a travesty of the personal realities of human life. As Fairbairn's patient protested: 'What I want is a father' so Fairbairn concluded that 'the ultimate goal of the libido is the object.'

As Guntrip also notes, Fairbairn, in a contradistinction to Klein, places great emphasis on the external facts of the child's real-life object relations as the cause of psychopathology. In this conception, the crucial individuals in the child's immediate early environment are at the root of psychopathology a view that is parallel in the later work of Kohut.

Fairbairn's developmental theory begins with a stage of infantile dependence wherein the mouth is the libidinal organ and the maternal breast the libidinal object. Infantile dependence proceeds through a transitional stage to mature dependence wherein ego and object are fully differentiated and the individual is capable of valuing the object for its own sake. Fairbairn (1956) states: 'This process of development is characterized and characterized (a) by the gradual abandonment of an original object relationship based upon primary identification, and (b) by the gradual adoption of an object relationship based upon differentiation of the object. The gradual change that thus occurs in the nature of the object relation is accompanied by a gradual change in libidinal aim, whereby an original oral, sucking, incorporating and predominantly 'taking' aim comes to be replaced by a mature, non-incorporating and predominantly 'giving' aim compatible with developed genital sexuality.' In this view schizophrenia and depression are, in part, at least, a consequence of disturbances of development during the stage of infantile dependence. Obsessional, paranoid, hysterical and phobic symptoms arise from attempts by the ego to deal with difficulties arising over object relationships during the transitional stage based on 'endopsychic situations that have resulted from the internalization of an object with which the ego has had relations hips during the stage of infantile dependence.'

For Fairbairn (1952) there is no reason to internalize a Satisfying object, 'being of so extreme a degree or quality as previously characterized or specified, is such, it is always the 'bad' object (i.e., at this stage, the unsatisfying object) that is internalized in the first stance; the difficulty to attach any meaning to the primary internalization of a 'good' object that is both satisfying and amenable from the infant's point of view. These are those, of course, who would argue that it would be natural for the infant, when in a state of deprivation, to internalize the good object on the wish-fulfilment principle, but, as it seems, internalization of objects is essentially a measure of coercion and it is not a satisfying object, but the unsatisfying object that the infant seeks to coerce. That is to say, 'The 'satisfying object' and 'unsatisfying object', are warranted for that which upon such considerations that, in this connection, the connection, in terms 'good object' and 'bad objects' tend to be misleading. They tend to be misleading because they are liable to be understood in the sense of 'desired object' and 'undesired object' respectfully. There can be no doubt, however, that a bad (understood as unsatisfying) object maybe desirous. Nonetheless, it is just because the infant's bad object is desired as well as felt to be that it is 'internalized.'

Fairbairn conceptualizes this unsatisfying object, one that frustrates and one that tempts. In order for the infant to deal with a now internalized intolerable situation, he splits the internal bad object into two—an exciting object and a frustrating object and represses both. As repression of objects proceed, the ego becomes divided, the original unitary ego is split and it is the relationship of the ego to these introjected objects, that is the cause of intrapsychic conflict and therefore pathological.

For Fairbairn, the presence of ego, the beginning of life replaces the classical view of undifferentiated id impulses, out of which structure will develop and this ego is object-directed. Ernest Jones (1952) summarizes Fairbairn's position: 'If it were possible to condense Fairbairn's new ideas into one sentence, it might run somewhat as follows. 'Instead of starting, as Freud did, from stimulation of the nervous system proceeding from excitation of various erotogenous zones and internal tension arising from monadic activity, Fairbairn starts at the centre of the personality, the ego, and depicted of its striving and difficulties, in its endeavour to reach an object where it may find support.

Impulses for Fairbairn, repression is merely the dynamic aspect of ego-structure and a radically reformulating of Freud's tripartite structural view of the mind is undertaken. The concept of the psychosexual stage is reformulated: '[Abraham] made the general mistake of conferring the status of libidinal phases upon what are really the techniques employed by the individual in his object-relationships.'

Fairbairn's work is a radical departure from classical theory. In its emphasis on the importance of early object relationships and the profound impact on the child's environment upon psychological development and psychopathologic transformations, it possesses close parallels with the later theoretical formulations of Kohut.

Heinz Kohut's clinical work with narcissistic disturbances (1971) led him to postulate a separate narcissistic line of development occurring alongside psychosexual and ego development. As his theory evolved, he developed a complete self-psychology

(1977) and abandoned concepts of instinctual drives as primary. His conceptualization of the development of the 'self' has to be seen as an object relation theory and within it there are strong echoes associated of the works of Fairbairn, particularly in its environmentalist approach, namely, that early actual object relations are central to the development of the personality and of the self. Kohut's theory of therapy also possesses close analogies to the concepts of Winnicott and Fairbairn by providing in the treatment situation a 'good object' for the patient in the person of the therapist who will be internalized and thus mitigate or repair deficits in the structure of the self-resulting from inadequate early parenting.

Edith Jacobson (1954) attempted to extend the instinctual model of the mind to encompass a fuller and better understanding of the development of both the 'self' and 'object relations.' Working within the classical psychoanalytic tradition, she views the original 'primary narcissistic state' of the newborn baby as a condition of diffuse dispersion of instinctual forces within a wholly undifferentiated psychic organization. In her conception, the libidinal and aggressive drives develop out of this state of undifferentiated physiological energy. Jacobson sees the discharge of psychic energy to the inside or the outside as crucial to an understanding of early infantile narcissism. She postulates that, from birth on, the infant possesses channels of discharge of psychic energy to the outside, (i.e., the mother's breast) which are the precursors of later object-related discharge. She views the building up of stable self, and objects representation cathected with libidinal energy as a central developmental undertaking. Like its primitive object image, the child's concept of self is initially unstable: 'Emerging from sensations hardly distinguishable from perceptions of the gratifying part-object, it is first fused and confused with the object image and is composed of a constantly changing series of self-images that reflect the incessant fluctuations of the primitive mental state.

In an illuminating statement in the relationship of unconscious fantasy to self and object relationships she observes that unpleasurable memories are dealt with by infantile repressions that thus eliminate a large part of the unacceptable aspects of the self and the outside world. The lacunae that are left are filled in by distortions or elaborations of the ego's defence system. Repressed fantasies will then lend current self and object representations: 'the colouring of past infantile images.' An example, which Jacobson provides of the dramatic phenomenon of infantile emotional experience preventing the formation of a correct body image is the persistence in a woman of the ubiquitous unconscious fantasy that their genitalia, as such, are castrated and accompanied by a simultaneous denial and developmental placements of illusionary penis fantasies.

Energid concepts remain central to Jacobson's thinking for she views the libido as moving from love objects to the self and from the self to love objects during early developmental stages. Healthy ego functioning in her view requires adequate, evenly distributed, a constant, libidinous cathexis of both object and that of self-representation. Differing drastically from Melanie Klein, Jacobson places the building up of self and object-representations firmly within the classical schemata of psychosexual development rather than telescoping them backward to early infancy. Thus, at first, the infant can barely discriminate between pleasurable sensations and the objects that provide them. Only with the increasing maturation of perception can gratifications or frustrations become associated with the object. The unpleasurable experiences of deprivation and separation from the love object give rise to fantasies of incorporation of the gratifying object, expressing a wish or reestablish union with the gratifying mother, a desire that Jacobson notes never ceases to play a part in one's emotional life. She states: 'Thus the earliest wishful fantasies of merging and being one with the mother (breast) is the foundations on which all future types of identifications are built . . . The hungry infant's longing for oral gratification is the origin of the first primitive type of identification, an identification achieved by refusion of self and object images and founded on wishful fantasises or oral incorporations of the love object.'

A gradual transition from fantasies of total incorporation to partial incorporation occurs with development marking the change from a desire for complete union to a wish to become like the mother. Jacobson views the internal object world as undergoing constant fluctuation during this period with libido and aggression moving from the love object to the self and back again, while self and object images as well as images of different objects undergo temporary fusions and separation, the mental life of the preoedipal child are dominated by magical fantasies, aspects of which persist into later life. Jacobson makes the point that it is necessary to distinguish between external objects and their endopsychic representations clearly and she criticizes Melanie Klein for failing to distinguish these mental representations from those of the self.

As growth proceeds instinctual striving stimulates the development of identifications overall. As the boy discovers sexual difference, his father becomes the main object of identification. As the ego evolves their identifications and object relations, of self and object representations. With the resolution of the oedipus complex and consequent superego formation. Jacobson sees the mental representations of the self and object world as taking on a lasting form. These in turn profoundly affect aspects of the personality and the manner in which the individual views himself and the world. Jacobson states: 'With full maturation and the achievement of instinctual mastery the representations of the self and of the object world overall, the representations of the self and of the object world usually acquire a final, characteristic configuration. When we compare and confront these formations with each other we find that in a normal person they have what may be called 'complementaries,' qualities that display a prominent aspect of his personality. When we characterize somebody, for instance, as an 'optimist' we mean that he regards himself as a lucky person, that he expects to be always successful and to gain gratifications easily, and that he views the world in a complementary way: As bound to be really pleasurable and to treat him well. In harmony with these concepts he will be a person inclined to be hopeful, gay, and in good spirits. By contrast, the 'pessimist' will experience the world as a constant source of harm, disappointment and failure, and himself accordingly as a poor devil forever apt to be deprived and hurt; consequently, the level of his mood will be preponderantly low. These examples show that, in a mature individual, these complementarities, and the qualities of his object-and self-representations reflect and define his fundamental position in relation to the world. The fact that in the course of life we may undergo further radical changes indicating that even after maturation and stabilization our concept of the object world and our own self may be profoundly influenced and altered by our life experiences and the biological stages through which we pass.

Kernberg (1979) notes that Jacobson's developmental model is the only comprehensive object relations theory that links the child's development of object relations, defence mechanisms, and instinctual vicissitudes with Freud's psychic apparatus of ego, id and superego. Hence, it represents the furthest extension to date of a classical psychoanalysis into the fields of object relations theory.

# CHAPTER ONE

# Instinct Versus Relationships

Freud's 'Three Essays on the Theory of Sexuality,' is a revolutionary work rivalling in magnitude his 'Interpretation of Dreams.' It is hard to imagine today the impact caused by his presentation of the unfolding of infantile sexuality and the relationship of the child's polymorphous perversity to the sexual aberrations and normal sexuality. His conception has become so much a part of the fabric of psychoanalytic thought and our surrounding intellectual culture that the radical and explosive nature of his theories, which overturned certain cherished beliefs in the society of the time, is often forgotten.

In 'The Psychogenesis of manic-depressive State' expounds the view of the centrality of the infantile depressive position in the normal development of the child's world of internal objects. In this view, failure to traverse this developmental stage successfully predisposes the individual to manic-depressive illness. Before the development of the depressive position in the child the paranoid-schizoid position dominates. The assumption is made by Klein that, from birth, the ego has the capacity to experience anxiety, to use defence mechanisms and to form object relations. At the beginning of life, the primary object is the breast, is split in two, the good object and persecutor one. The fantasy of the good object receives reinforcement by gratifying experiences from the mother while a fantasy of the bad object is reinforced by experiences of frustration and pain. The infant's anxiety in this stage, according to

Klein, is that the bad object will overwhelm and destroy the good object and the self.

When good experiences are predominant over bad, the child acquires a belief in the goodness of the object and the self. Fear of the persecuting object declines, and the split between good and bad objects decreases. The child develops greater tolerance for its own aggression and has less need to project it outwards. Internal objects become increasingly integrated and there is growing differentiation between self and object, thus setting the stage for the onset of the depressive position. The mother is now recognized as a whole object who is separate from the child. Anxieties then centre on ambivalence and the child's fear that his aggressive impulses have destroyed or will destroy the object that he is totally dependent upon. Introjective mechanisms increase, in response to the need to posses the object and protect it from his aggression. The child is now in the depressive position. The fear that the good object has been destroyed or lost leads to mourning and guilt. Simultaneously, because of increasing identification with the good object, preservation of it becomes synonymous with the survival of the self.

Klein develops the themes of the evolving internal object world and its vicissitudes to explain depression, suicide, and mania. There is a compelling quality to her interpretations of clinical material, not withstanding the severe criticism she has received for her theoretical views. Guntrip (1969) notes that Kleinian theory implies fixed limits to what psychotherapy can achieve because of her postulate of a permanent destructive urge (the death instinct) in all of us, which cannot be analyzed. The implication is, as he notes, that our very nature is intrinsically bad. For all that many of Klein's conceptualizations have been criticized, Zetzel (1956) notes that her contributions to psychoanalytic theory are considerable, namely, her recognition of the role of aggression in early mental life, the crucial importance of early object relations, and the role of anxiety as a spur to development.

While rejecting Klein's view that internal reality is predominant and that adaptation to external reality is dependent on mastery of the inner world, Fairbairn makes creative use of her conception of an internal object world.

What is more, he reverses Freud's theory of libidinal development by postulating that libidinal pleasure serves fundamentally as a sign to the object rather than its opposite. The object relationship determines the libidinal attitude, not the reverse. For him libidinal development depends upon the degree to which objects are incorporated and the nature of the methods used to deal with incorporated objects. In radical opposition to classical psychoanalytic theory, Fairbairn downplays the importance of the oedipus complex. He sees it as a relatively superficial phenomenon on which represents merely a differentiation of the single object of the late oral phases of development into two, one being an accepted object, identified with one of the parents, and the other being a rejected object, identified with the remaining parent. Psychopathology is now conceptualized in terms of the disturbance of object relationships during development and not in terms of intrapsychic conflict between id and ego.

Furthermore, Fairbairn applies his psychology of object relationships to a revision of the classic theory of repression. For him, the nature of the repressed lies in the relationship of the ego to bad internalized objects. Unlikely Freud who viewed the repressed as consisting of intolerably guilty impulses or intolerably unpleasant memories, Fairbairn sees the repressed as consisting of intolerably bad internalized objects. In his theory of therapy, Fairbairn conceives of the psychotherapist as an exorcist who casts out the devil (the bad objects) from the patient's unconscious, by providing himself as a powerful good object who gives the patient sufficient sense of security to allow the terrifying bad objects slowly to emerge on closer examination.

For Fairbairn the development of the individual hinges on the vicissitudes of object relationships and not on the vicissitudes of the drives. However, as Eagle (1984) notes, his view of object seeking was primary and was intrinsically biological as the sexual and aggressive drives are conceived of in classical instinct theory, implies the presence of an instinct concept in the theoretical formulation, an object seeking instinct.

Arlow's paper provides an avenue to understanding the determinants of object choice. He takes issue with the view of any object relations theorists who feel that the earliest interaction between the child and the mother determines the quality of subsequent love relationships. While acknowledging that the earliest object relationship with the mother has an influence on patterns of loving, he does not feel it is necessarily decisive. He highlights the complexity of patterns of loving and object choice that he sees as determined primarily by persistent unconscious fantasies. Through clinical examples he illustrates the interrelationship of defence, object relations and instinctual gratification in deciding the nature of love and hence objects choice in any given individual.

Arlow emphasizes the concept of the object as an intrapsychic mental representation highly cathected with the libido. This mental representation grows out of a remembered group of pleasurable sensations that the individual wishfully attempts to reconstruct. He makes the important point that object relations and interpersonal relations are by no means in saying identical. For Arlow it is the effect of unconscious fantasy wishes connected with specific mental representations of objects that distort and affects the quality of interpersonal relations. During childhood, the memory traces of pleasurable sensation connected with an external person become organized into a memory connection with an external person becoming organized into a memory structure, a mental representation of a person, i.e., the 'object.' Mental representations connected with pain may also develop and it is in this sense that Arlow understands Klein's thesis of good and bad objects. Later in development, the disparate mental representations are fused into the concept of an external person, but this organized concept, made up of an amalgam of earlier object representations may dissolve regressively. In this fashion, Arlow interprets the concept of 'splitting.'

Arlow's paper is a sophisticated extension of Freud's original ideas, promulgated in his 'Three Essays on the Theory of Sexuality,' and now places within the structural theory of the psychic apparatus. The pleasure principle and hence instinctual gratifications are dominant patterns of loving and are determined by several types of persistent unconscious fantasies, derived from different times in the individual's relations to important objects of the past. Love relations may change at different states of the individual's life reflecting the unconscious conflict that the individual is trying to resolve at that moment. Thus object relationship in Arlow's view is firmly placed in a matrix of drive conflict, a thesis that stands in contrast to the view of Fairbairn.

# REFERENCES

* Eagle M. N. (1984). Recent Developments in Psychoanalysis. NY. McGraw-Hill
* Guntrip H. (1969). Schizoid Phenomena, Object Relations and the Self. NY: International Universities Press.
* Zetzel E. (1956), "An approach to the relation between concept and content in psychoanalytic theory (with special reference to the work of Melaine Klein and her followers)" Psychoanalytic Study of the Child, 11: 990-121

# CHAPTER TWO

# The Psychogenesis of Manic-Depressive States

Melanie Klein, in her earlier writings contain the account of a phase of 'sadism' at its zenith, through which children passes during the first year of life. In the very first months of the baby's existence it has sadistic impulses directed, not only against its mother's breast, but also against the inside of her body: scooping it out, devouring the contents, destroying it by every means which sadism can suggest. The development of the infant is governed by the mechanisms of introjection and projection. From the beginning the ego introjects objects 'good' and 'bad' for both of which its mother's breast is the prototype—for good objects when the child obtains it and for bad when it fails him. But it is because the baby project its own aggression onto these objects' that it feels that to be 'bad' and not in that they frustrate its desire: the child conceives of them as actually dangerous—persecutors who it fear's will devour it, scoop out the inside of its body, cut it to pieces, poison it—in short, compassing its destruction by all the means which sadism can be a device. These imagoes, which are a fantastically distorted picture of the real objects upon which they are based, are installed by it not only in the outside world but, by the process of incorporation, also within the ego. Therefore, quite little children pass through anxiety-situations (and react to them with defence-mechanisms), the content of which is comparable to that of the psychosis of adults.

One of the earliest methods of defence against the dread of persecutors, whether conceived of as existing in the external world or internalized, is that of scotomization, the denial of psychic reality; this may result in a considerable restriction of the mechanisms of introjection and projection and in the denial of external reality, and it forms the basis of the most severe psychoses. Very soon, too, the ego tries to defend itself against internalized persecutors by the processes of expulsion and projection. At the same time, since the dread of internalized objects is by no means extinguished with their projection, the ego marshal's against the persecutors inside the body the same forces as it employs against those in the outside world. These anxiety-contents and defence-mechanisms form the basis of paranoia, in the infantile dread of magicians, which, evil beasts, and so on, we detect something of this same anxiety, but it has already undergone projection and modification. Moreover, is that infantile psychotic anxiety, in particular paranoid anxiety, is bound and modified by the obsessional mechanisms that make their appearance very early.

Collocated with manic states are various degrees and forms, including the slightly hypomanic states that occur in normal persons. The analysis of depressive and manic features in normal children and adults also proved very instructive.

According to Freud and Abraham, the fundamental process in melancholia is the loss of the loved object. The real loss of a real object, or some similar situation having the same significance, results in the object becoming installed within the ego. Owing, however, to an excess of cannibalistic impulse in the subject, this introjection miscarries and consequence is illness.

Now, why is it that the process of introjection is so specific for melancholia? Because the main difference between incorporation in paranoia and in melancholia is connected with changes in the relation of the subject to the object, though it is also a question of a change in the constitution of the introjecting ego. According to Edward Glover, the ego, at first but loosely organized, consists of a considerable number of ego-nucleins In his view, in the first place an oral ego-nucleus and later an anal ego-nucleus predominate over the others. In this very early phase, in which oral sadism plays a prominent part and which is the basis of schizophrenia, the ego's power of identifying itself with its objects is as yet small, partly because it is itself still incorporated and partly because the introjected objects are still mainly partial objects, which it equates with faces.

In paranoia the characteristic defences are chiefly aimed at annihilating the 'persecutors,' while anxiety on the ego's account occupies a prominent place in the picture. As the ego becomes more fully organized, the internalized imagoes will approximate more closely to reality and the ego will identify itself more fully with 'good' objects. The dread of persecution, which was at first felt on the ego account, now relates to the good object as well and from now on preservation of the good object is regarded as synonymous with the survival of the ego.

Grasping tightly on or upon this development goes a change of the highest importance, namely, from a partial object-relation to the relation to a complete object. Through this step the ego arrives at a new position, which forms the foundation of that situation called the loss of the loved object. Not until the object is loved as a whole can its loss be felt as a whole.

With this change in the relation to the object, new anxiety-contents make their appearance and a change takes place in the mechanisms of defence. The development of the libido also is decisively influenced. Paranoid anxiety least the objects sadistically destroy, should they be a source of poison and danger inside the subject's body causes him, in spite of the vehemence of his oral-sadistic onslaught, at the same time to be profoundly mistrustful of them while yet incorporating them.

This leads to a weakening of oral fixation. One manifestation of this may be observed in the difficulties very young children often show in regard to eating which, perhaps, always have a paranoid root. As a child (or an adult) identifies himself more fully with a good object, the libidinal urge urges increase: he develops a greedy love and desire to devour this object and the mechanism of introjection is reinforced. Besides, he finds himself constantly impelled to repeat the incorporation of a good object, partly because dreads that he has fortified it by his cannibalism—, i.e., the repetition of the act is designed to test the reality of his fears and disproves them—and partly because he fears internalized persecutors against whom he requires a good object to help him. In this stage the ego is more than ever driven both by love and by need to introject the object.

Another stimulus for an increase of introjection is the fantasy that loved object maybe preserved in safety inside oneself. In this case the dangers of the inside are projected onto the external world.

If, however, consideration for the object increase, and a better acknowledgement of psychic reality sets in, the anxiety least the object should be destroyed in the process of introjection, it leads—as Abraham has described—to various disturbances of the function of introjection.

There is, furthermore, a deep anxiety as to the dangers that await the object inside the ego. It could not be safely maintained there, as the inside is felt to be a dangerous and poisonous place in which the loved object would perish. In that, we see one of the situations that has been described as fundamental for 'the loss of the loved object,' the situation, namely, when the ego becomes fully identified with its good, internalized objects, and at the same time becomes aware of its own incapacity to protect and preserve them against the internalized, persecuting objects and the id. This anxiety is psychologically justified.

For the ego, when it becomes fully identified with the object; does not abandon its earlier defence-mechanisms? According to Abraham's hypothesis, the annihilation and expulsion of the object—processes characteristic of the earlier anal level—initiate the depressive mechanism. If this is so, it confirmed the notion of the genetic connection between paranoia and melancholia. Such that the paranoiac mechanism of destroying the objects (whether inside the body or in the outside world) by every means which oral, urethral and anal sadism can command, persists, but in a lesser degree and with a certain modification due to the change in the subject's relation to his object. Even so, the dread least the good object should be expelled along with the bad causes the mechanisms of expulsion and projection to lose value. We know that, at this stage, the ego makes a greater use of introjection of the good object as a mechanism of defence. This is associated with another important mechanism: that of making reparation to the object. In certain works the detailing concept of restoration and that it is far more than a mere reaction-formation. The ego feels impelled (impelled by its identification with the good object) to make restitution for all the sadistic attacks that it has launched on the object. When a well-marked cleavage attacks good and bad objects have been attained, the subject attempt to restore the former, making good the restoration to every contingent in dealings of his sadistic attacks, but, the ego cannot as yet believe enough in the benevolence of the object and in its own capacity makes restitution. On the other hand, through its identification with a good object and through the other mental advance that this implies, the ego finds itself forced to a fuller recognition of psychic reality, and this exposed it to fierce conflicts. Some of its objects—an indefinite number—are persecutors to it, ready to devour and do violence to it. In all sorts of ways they endanger both the ego and the good object. Every injury inflicted in fantasy by the child upon its parents (primarily from hate and secondarily in a self-defence), every act of violence committed by one object upon another (in particular the destructive, sadistic coitus of the parents, which it regards as yet, another consequence of its own sadistic wishes)—all this is played out, both in the outside world and, since the ego is constantly absorbing into itself, and, the whole external world, within the ego as well. Now, however, all these processes are viewed as a perpetual source of danger both to the good object and to the ego.

It is true that, now that good and bad objects are more clearly differentiated, the subject's hate is directed rather against the latter, while his love and his attempts at reparation are more focussed on the former; But the excess of his sadism, and anxiety acts as a check to this advance in his mental development. Every external or internal stimulus (e.g., every real frustration) is fraught with the utmost danger: Not only bad objects but also the good ones thus, menaced by the id, for every access of hate or anxiety may temporarily abolish the differentiation and thus result in a 'loss of the loved object.' And it is not only the vehemence of the subject's uncontrollable hatred but that of his love too which imperils the object. For at this stage of his development loving an object and devouring it is very closely connected. A little child that believes, when its mother disappears, that it has eaten her up and destroyed her (whether from motives of love or of hate) is tormented by anxiety both for her and for the good mother that it has absorbed into itself.

It now becomes plain why, at this phase of development, the ego feels itself constantly menaced in its possession of internalized good objects. It is full of anxiety least such objects should die. Both in children and adults suffering from depression, finding that dread is harbouring dying or dead objects (especially the parents) inside one and an identification of the ego with objects in this condition.

From the very beginning of psychic development there is a constant correlation of real objects with those installed within the ego. It is for this reason that the anxiety that subscribes to the manifestation itself in a child's exaggeration fixation to its mother or whoever looks after it. The absence of the mother arouses in the child's anxiety least it should be handed over to bad objects, external and internalized, either because of her death or because of her return in the guise of a 'bad' mother.

Both cases signify to it that it has lost its loved mother, from which the fact that dread of the loss of the 'good', internalized object becomes a perpetual source of anxiety least the real mother should die. On the other hand, every experience that suggests the loss of the real loved object stimulates the dread of losing the internalized one too.

Nonetheless, the loss of the loved object takes place during that phase of development in which the ego makes the transition from partial to total incorporation of the object. Having now described the situation of the ego in that place, in which the processes that subsequently become defined as 'loss of the loved object' are determined by the subject's sense of failure (during weaning and in the periods that precede and follow it) to secure his good, internalized object, i.e., to posses himself of it. One reason for his failure is that he has been unable to over come his paranoid dread of internalized persecutors.

At this point we are confronted with a question of importance for our whole theory. Such that the direct influence of the early processes of introjection upon both normal and pathological development is very much more momentous, and in some respects other, than has hitherto commonly been accepted in psycho-analytical circles.

According to our views, even the earliest incorporated object's from the basis of the Superego and enter its structure. The question is by no means a merely theoretical one. As we study the relations of the early infantile ego to its internalized objects and to the id, and come to understand the gradual changes these relations undergo, we obtain a deeper insight into the specific anxiety-situations through which the ego passes and the specific defence-mechanisms that it develops as it becomes more highly organized. Viewed from this standpoint in our experience we find that we arrive at a complete understanding of the earliest phases of psychic development, of the structure of the Superego and of the genesis of psychotic diseases. For where we deal with aetiology it seems essential to regard the libido-disposition not merely as such, but also to consider it in connection with the subject's earliest relations to his internalized and external objects, a consideration that implies an understanding of the defence-mechanisms developed by the ego gradually in dealing with its varying anxiety-situations.

If we accept this view of the formation of the Superego, its relentless severity in the case of the melancholic become more intelligible. The persecutions and demands of bad internalized objects, the attacks of such objects upon another especially that represented protect and placate them within the ego, with the resultant hatred of the id; the constant certainty as the 'goodness' of a good object, which causes it to be readily to become transformed into a bad one—all these factors combine to produce in the ego a sense of being a prey to contradictory and impossible claims from within, a condition that is felt as a bad conscience. That is to say: The earliest utterances of conscience are associated with persecution by having objects. The very word 'gnawing of conscience' (Gewissensbisse) testifies to the relentless 'persecution' of conscience and to the fact that it is originally conceived of as devouring its victim.

Among the various internal demands that go to make up the severity of the Superego in the Superego in the melancholic, least his urgent need to comply with the very strict demands of the 'good' objects. It is this part of the picture only—namely, the cruelty of the 'good,' i.e., loved, objects within—which has been recognized hitherto by general analytic opinion, namely, in the relentless severity of the Superego in the melancholic. But, it is only by looking at the whole relation of the ego to its fantastically bad objects as well as to its good objects, only by looking at the whole picture of the internal situation that in having tried, is that we can understand the slavery to which the ego submits when complying with the extremely cruel demands and admonitions of its loved object that has become installed within the ego. Even so, the ego endeavours to keep the good apart from the bad, and the real from the fantasy objects. The result is a conception of extremely bad and extremely perfect objects, which is to say, its loved objects are in many ways intensely moral and exacting. At the same time, since the ego cannot really keep its good and bad objects apart in its mind, some of the cruelty of the bad objects and of the id becomes related to the good objects and this then again, increase the severity of their demands. These strict demands serve the purpose of supporting the ego in it s fight against its uncontrollable hatred and its bad attacking objects, with whom the ego is partly identified. The stronger the anxiety is of losing the loved objects, restoration becomes the stricter will grow the demands that are associated with the Superego.

Having endeavoured to show that the difficulties that the ego experiences when it passes on to the incorporation of whole objects proceeds from it as yet imperfect capacity for mastering, by means of its new defence-mechanisms, the fresh anxiety-contents arising out of this advance in its development.

So far, I am aware of how difficult it is to draw a sharp line between the anxiety-contents and feeling of the paranoiac and those of the depressive, since they are so closely linked with each other. But they can be distinguished one from the other if, as a criterion of differentiation, one considers whether the persecution-anxiety is brave related to the preservation of the ego—in which case it is paranoiac—to the preservation of the good internalized objects with which the ego is depressive as a whole. In the latter case—which is the casse of the depressive—the anxiety and feelings of suffering are of a much more complex nature the anxiety, least, the good objects and with them the ego should be destroyed, or that they are in a state of disintegration, is interwoven with continuous and desperate efforts to save the good objects both internalized and external.

It seems, nonetheless, when the ego has introjected the object as a whole and has established a better relationship both the external world and to real people is it able fully to realize that disaster created through its sadism and especially through its cannibalism, and to feel distressed about it. This distress is related not only to the past but to the present as well, since at this early stage of development the sadism is in full swing. It needs a fuller identification with the loved object, and a fuller recognition of its value, for the ego to become aware of that state if disintegration to which it has deduced and is continuing to reduce its loved object. The ego then finds itself confronted with the physical fact that its loved objects are in a state of the dissolution—in bits—and the despair, remorse and anxiety deriving from this recognition are at the bottom of numerous anxiety-situations,. To quote only a few of them: There is anxiety how to put the bits together in the right way and at the right time; how to pick out the good bits and do away with the bad ones; how to bring the object to life when it has been put together; and there is the anxiety of being interfered within this task by bad objects and by one's own hatred, and so on.

Anxiety-situations of this kind are found to be at the bottom, not only of depression, but of all in inhibitions of work. The attempts to save the loved object, to repair and restore it, attempts that in the state of depression are coupled with despair, since the ego doubts its capacity to achieve this restoration, are determining factors for all sublimations and the whole of the ego-development. In this connection, least of mention, the specific importance for sublimation of the bits to which the loved object has been reduced and the effort to put them together. It is a 'perfect' object that is in pieces; thus the effort to undo the state of disintegration to which bit has been reduced presupposes the necessity to make it beautiful and 'perfect.' The idea of perfection is, moreover, so compelling because it disproves the idea of disintegration. In some patient's who had turned away from their mother in dislike or hate, or used in their minds, nevertheless, a beautiful picture of the mother, but one that was felt to be a picture of her only, not her real self. The real object was felt to be unattractive—really an injured, incurable and form real objects but had never been given up. And played a great part in the specific ways of their sublimation.

It appears that the desire for perfection is rooted in the depressive anxiety of disintegration, which is thus great importance in all sublimation.

And to say again, the ego comes to a realization of its love for a good object, a whole object and in addition a real object, together with an overwhelming feeling of guilt toward it. Full identification with the object based on the libidinal attachment, first to the breast, then to the whole person, goes hand in hand with anxiety for it (of its disintegration), with guilt and remorse, with a sense of responsibility for preserving its entirety against persecutors and that of the id, and with sadness relating to expectations of the impending loss of it. These emotions, whether conscious or unconscious, are in between the essential and fundamental elements of the feelings we call love.

In this connection, the familiarity with the self-reproaching of the depressive that represents reproached against the object. But to mind, the ego's hate of the id, which is paramount in this phase, accounts even more for its feelings of unworthiness and despair than on its reproaches against the object. In finding that these reproaches and the hate against objects are secondarily increased as a defence against the hatred of the id, which is even more unbearable. In the last analysis it is the ego's unconscious knowledge that the hate is to be. But also, there is as well the love, that may be at any time get the upper hand (the ego's anxiety of being carried away by the id and so destroying the loved object), which brings about the sorrow, feelings of guilt and the despair, which underlie grief. This anxiety is also responsible for the doubt of the goodness of the loved object. As Freud has pointed out, doubt is in reality a doubt of one's own love, as a man who doubts of his own love, is in reality, a doubt of one's own love, or rather must, doubts every lesser thing.

The paranoiac, in that he has introjected a whole and real object, but gas not been to achieve a full identification with it, or, if he has got as far as this, he has not been able to maintain it. To mention a few of the reasons that are responsible for this failure: The persecution-anxiety is too great; but suspicions and anxieties of a fantastic nature stand in the way of a full and stable introjection of a good object and a real one. In as far as it has been introjected, there is little capacity to maintain it as a good object, since doubts and suspicions of all kinds will soon turn the loved object again into a persecutor. Thus his relationship to whole objects and the real world is still influenced by his early relation to internalized part-objects and faeces as persecutors and may again give way to the latter.

However, it seems characteristic of the paranoiac that, though, on account of his persecution-anxiety and his suspicions, he develops a very strong and acute power of observation of the external world and of real objects, this observation and his sense of reality are nevertheless, distorted, since his persecution-anxiety makes him look at people mainly from the point of view of whether they are persecutors or not. Where the persecution-anxiety for the ego is in the ascendable reference to his character, and a full and stables identification with another object, in the sense of looking at it and understanding it as it really is, and a full capacity for love, are not possible.

Another important reason that the paranoiac cannot maintain his whole-object relation is that while the persecution-anxiety and the anxiety for himself are still so strong in operation he cannot endure the additional burden of anxieties for a loved object and, besides, the feelings of guilt and remorse that accompany this depressive position. Moreover, in this position he can make far less use of projection, for fear of expelling his good objects as so losing them, and, on the other hand, for fear of injuring good external objects by expelling what is bad from within himself.

Thus, we see that the sufferings connected with the depressive position thrust him back to the paranoiac position. Nevertheless, though he has retreated from it, the depressive position has been reached and therefore, the liability to depression is always there. This accounts, as for the fact that we frequently need depression along with severe paranoia as well as in milder cases.

If we compare the feelings of the paranoiac with those of the depressive in regard to disintegration, one can see that characteristically the depressive is filled with sorrow and anxiety for the object, which he would strive to unite again into a whole, while to the paranoiac the disintegration object is mainly a multitude of persecutors, since each piece is growing again into a persecutor. The conception of the dangerous fragments to which the object is reduced seems to be in keeping with the introjection of part-objects that are equated with faeces (Abraham), and with the anxiety of a multiple of an internal persecutor to whom, the introjection of many part-objects and the multitude of dangerous faeces give rises.

Under the due considerations for that which the distinctions between the depressive from the point of view of their different relations to loved objects. The anxiety of absorbing dangerous substances destructive to one's inside will thus be paranoiac, while the anxiety of destroying the external good object by introducing bad substances from outside into it will be depressive. Again, the anxiety of leading an external good object into danger within oneself and incorporating it as a depressive one. On the other hand, in cases with strong paranoiac features, as to the phantasies of luring an external object into one's inside, which was regarded as a cave full of dangerous monsters', and so on. As we can see, the paranoiac reason for an intensification of the introjection-mechanism, while the depressive employs this mechanism so characteristically, as we know, for the purposes of incorporating a good object.

Considering now hypochondriacal symptoms in this comparative way, the pains and other manifestations that in fantasy results from the attacks of internal bad objects within against the ego are typically paranoid. The symptoms that derives, on the other hand, from the attacks of bad internal objects and the id against good ones, i.e., an internal warfare in which the ego is identified with the sufferings of the good objects, are typically depressive.

For instance, a patient who has been told as a child that he hade tapeworms (which he himself never saw) connected the tapeworms inside him with his greediness. In his analysis he had fantasies that a tapeworm was eating its way through his body and a strong anxiety of cancer came to the fore. The patient, who suffered from hypochondriacal and paranoid anxieties, was very suspicious of the therapist, and, among other things, suspected the therapist for being allied with people who were hostile toward him. At this time he dreamed that a detective was arresting a hostile and persecuting person and putting this person in prison. But then the detective proved unreliable and became the accomplice of the enemy. The detective stood for the therapist and the whole anxiety was internalized and was connected with the tapeworm fantasy. The prison in which the enemy was kept was his own inside—actually the special part of his inside where the persecutor was to be confined. It became clear that the dangerous tapeworm (one of his associations was that the tapeworm is bisexual) represented the two parents in a hostile alliance (actually in intercourse) against him.

At the same time, the feelings and fantasies connected with his hypochondriacal pains changed. For instance, the patient felt anxiety that the cancer would make its way through the lining of his stomach; but now it appeared that, while he feared for his stomach, he really wanted to protect the therapist—actually the internalized mother—whom he felt was being attacked by the father's penis and by his own id (the cancer). Another time, the patient had fantasies connected with physical discomfort about an internal haemorrhage from which he would die. It became clear that the therapist was identified with the haemorrhage, the good blood representing the therapist. We must remember that, when the paranoid anxieties dominated and the therapist was mainly felt as a persecutor, this had been identified with the bad blood that was mixed with the diarrhea (with the bad father). Now the precious good blood represented the therapist—losing it meant the death of the therapist, which would imply his death. It became clear now that the cancer that he made responsible for the death of his loved object, as well as for his own, and which stood for the bad father's penis, was even more felt to be his own sadism, especially his greed. That is why he felt so unworthy and so much in despair.

After having attempted to differentiate between the anxiety-contents, feelings and defences at work in paranoia and those in the depressive states, such that the depressive state is based on the paranoid state and genetically derived from it. Considering the depressive state for being the result of a mixture of paranoid anxiety and of those anxiety-contents, distressed feelings and defences that are connected with the impending loss of the whole loved object. It seems that to introduce a term for those specific anxieties and defences might further the understanding of the structure and nature of paranoia as well as of the manic-depressive states.

As of taking to be in manic-depressives state that exists, be in it the normal, the neurotic, in manic-depressive or in mixed cases, there is always in it this specific grouping of anxieties, distressed feelings and different varieties of these defences, which has been described at full length.

If this point of view proves correct, we should be able to understand those very frequent cases where we are presented with a picture of mixed paranoiac and depressive trends, since we could then isolate the various elements of which it is composed.

The considerations that have been brought forward, concerning the depressive states that may lead us, in at least, to a better understanding of the still rather enigmatic reaction of suicide. According to the findings of Abraham and James Glover, a suicide is directed against the introjected object. But, while in committing suicide the ego intends to murder its bad object, so that, at the same time, it also aims at saving its loved object, internal or external. To put it shortly, in some cases the fantasies underlying suicide aim at preserving the internalized good objects and that part of the ego that is identified with good objects, and at destroying the other part of the ego that is identified with the bad objects and that of the id. Thus the ego is enabled to become united with its loved objects.

In other cases, suicide seems to be determined by the same type of fantasies, but relate to the external world and real objects, partly as substitutes for the internalized ones. As already stated, the subject hates not only his 'bad' objects, but his id as well, and vehemently. In committing suicide, his purpose may be to make a clean breach in his relation to the outside world because he desires to rid some real objects—or, the 'good' object that the whole world represent and which the ego is identified with—of himself, or that part of his ego that identified with his bad objects along with that of the id. At bottom, we receive in such a step his reaction to his own sadistic attack as on his mother's body, which to a little child is the first representative of the outside world. Hatred and revenge against the real (good) object also always play an important part in such a step, bu t it is precisely the uncontrollable dangerous hatred that is perpetually welling up to him from which the melancholic by his suicide is in part struggling to preserve his real objects.

Freud has stated that mania has for its basis the same contents as melancholia and is, in fact, a way of escape from that state. As, perhaps, that in mania the ego seeks refuges not only from melancholia but also from a paranoiac condition that it is unable to master. Its torturing and perilous dependence on its loved objects drive the ego to find freedom. But its identification with these objects is too profound to be renounced. On the other hand, the ego is pursued by its dread of bad objects and along with the id and, in its effort to escape from all these miseries, it belongs to different phases of development, are mutually incompatible.

The sense of omnipotence, is what first and foremost characterizes mania and, further (as Helene Deutsch has stated) mania is based on the mechanisms of denial, however, from Helene Deutsch in the following point. She holds that this 'denial' is connected with the phallic phase and the castration complex (in young women it is a denial of the lack of the penis); while observations have led to conclude that this mechanism of denial originates in that very early phase in which there undeveloped ego endeavours to defend itself from the most overpowering and profound anxiety of all, namely, it dread of an internalized persecutor and of the id. That is to say, that which is first of all denial is psychic reality and the ego may than go on to deny a great deal of external reality.

We know that scotomization may lead to the subject's becoming entirely cut off from reality, and to his complete inactivity. Ln mania, however, denial is associated with an overactivity, although this excess of activity, as Helene Deutsch pointed out, often bears no relation to any actual results achieved. Wherefore, to explain that in this state the source of the conflict is that the ego is unwilling and unable to renounce its good internal objects and yet endeavours to escape from the perils of dependence on them as well as from its bad objects. Its attempt to detach itself from an object without completely renouncing it seems to be conditioned by an increase in the ego's own strength. It succeeds in this compromise by denying the importance of its good objects and of the dangers with which it is menaced from its bad objects and the id. At the same time, however, it endeavours ceaselessly to master and control all its objects, and the evidence of this is its hyperactivity.

What to my view for mania is the utilization of the sense of omnipotence for the purpose of controlling and mastering objects. This is necessary for two reasons: (a) In order to deny the dread of them that is bearing experience, and (b) So that the mechanism (acquired in the previous—the depressive—position) of making reparation to the object may be carried through. By mastering his objects the manic person imagines he will prevent them not only from injuring himself but from being a danger to one another. His mastery is to enable him, particularly to prevent dangerous coitus between the parents he has internalized and their death within him. The manic defence assumes so many forms that it is, of course, not easy to postulate a general mechanism. Even so, we really have such a mechanism (though its varieties are infinite) in this mastery of the internalized parent's, while at the same time, the existence of this internal world is being depreciated and denied. Both in children and in adults have, perhaps, that where obsessional neurosis was the most powerful factor in the case, such mastery betokened as a forcible separation of two (or more) objects; whereas, where mania was in the ascendant, the patients have recourse to methods more violent. That is to say, the objects were killed, but since the subject was omnipotent, he supposes he could also immediately call them to life again. Keeping of this process as 'keeping them in suspended animation,' the killing corresponds to the defence-mechanism (retained from the earliest phase) of destruction of the object; the resuscitation corresponds to the reparation made to the object. In this position the ego effects a similar compromise in its relation to real objects. The hunger for objects, so characteristic of mania, indicates that the ego has retained one defence-mechanism of the depressive-position; the introjection of good objects. The manic subject denies the different forms of anxiety associated with this introjection (anxiety, which is to say, least that either he should introject as object, or else destroy his good objects by the process of introjection): His denial relates not merely to the impulses of the id but to his own concern for the object's safety. Thus we may suppose that the process by which ego and ego-ideal come to coincide, as Freud has shown that they do in mania is as follows. The ego incorporates the object in a cannibalistic way (the 'feast' as Freud calls it in his account of mania) but denies that it feels any concern for it. 'Surely,' argues the ego, 'it is not a matter of such great importance if this particular object is destroyed, there are so many others to be incorporated.' This disparagement of the object's importance and the contempt for it is, nonetheless, a specific characteristic of mania and enables the ego to effect that partial detachment that we observe side by side with its hunger for objects. Such detachments, which the ego cannot achieve in the depressive position, represents an advance, a fortifying of the ego in relation to its objects. But this advance is counteracted by the regressive mechanisms described which the ego at the same time employ in mania.

Then there are the dangers threatening from the id. If jealousy and hate stirred by some real frustration are to a great extent, he will again in his fantasy attack the internalized father with his burning excreta, and disturbing their intercourse, which gives rise to renewed anxiety. Either external or internal stimuli may increase his paranoid anxieties of internalized persecutors, if he then kills his father inside him together, the dead father becomes a persecutor of a special kind. We see this from the patient's remark (and the following associations) that if gas is extinguished by liquid, poison remains behind. As the paranoid position comes to the fore and the dead object within comes equated with faeces and flatus, that is, however, the paranoid position, which had been very strong in the patient at the beginning of his analysis, but is now greatly diminished, does not appear much in the dreams.

It is, nonetheless, that in the first few months of its life the child goes through paranoid anxieties related to 'bad' denying breasts, which are felt as external and internalized persecutors. From this relation to part-objects, and from their equation with faeces, springs at this stage as the fantastic and unrealistic nature of the child's relation to all other things; part of its body, people and things around it, which are at first but dimly perceived. The object-world of the child in the first two or three months of its life could be described as consisting of hostile and persecuting, or else of gratifying parts and portions of the real world. Before long, the child perceives more of the whole people of the mother, and this more realistic perception extends to the world beyond the mother. The fact that a good relation toward its mother and to the external world helps the baby to overcome its early paranoid anxieties and throws a new light on the importance of its earliest experiences. From its inception analysis has always laid stress on the importance of the child's early experiences, but it seems that only since we know more about the nature and contents of its early anxieties, and the continuous interplay between its experiences, and its fantasy-life, are we able fully to understand why the external factor is so important. But when this happens its sadistic fantasies and feelings, especially its cannibalistic ones, are at their height. At the same time it now experiences a change in bits of emotional attitude toward its mother. The child's libidinal fixation to the breast develops into feelings toward her as a person. Thus feelings both of a destructive and a loving nature are experiences toward one and the same object and this gives rise to deep and disturbing conflicts in the child's mind.

In the normal course of events the ego is faced at this point of its development—roughly between four and five months of age—with the necessity to acknowledge psychic reality as well as the external reality to a certain degree. It is thus made to realize that the loved object is at the same time the hated one, and in addition to this that the real objects and the imaginary figures, both external and internal, are bound up with each other. Even so, that in the quite small child there exists, in side by side with its relations to real objects—but on a different plane, as it was—relations to its unreal imago, both as excessively good and excessively bad figures and that these two kinds of object-relations intermingle and colour each other to an ever-increasing degree in the course of development. The first important steps as in this direction occur, when the child comes to know its mother as a whole person and become identified with her as a whole, real and a loved person. It is then that the depressive position—the characteristic of which has come to the fore. This position is stimulated and reinforced by the 'loss of the loved object' which the baby experiences over and over again when the mother's breast is taken away from it, and this loss reaches its climax during weaning. Sándor Radó has pointed out that 'the deepest fixation-point in the depressive disposition is to be found in the situation of threatened loss of love (Freud), more especially in the hunger situation of the sucking baby.' Referring to Freud's statement that in mania the ego is once more merged with the Superego in unity. Radó comes to the conclusion that 'this process is the faithful intrapsychic repetition of the experience of that fusing with the mother that takes place during drinking at her breast.' Wherefore, these statements differ in important points from the conclusions that Radó arrives at, especially about the indirect and circuitous way in which he thinks that guilt becomes connected with these early experiences. Such that the sucking period, when it comes to know its mother as a whole person and when it progresses from the introjection of part-objects to the introjection of the whole object, the infant experiences some of the feelings of guilt and remorse. Some of the pain that results from the conflict between love and uncontrollable hatred, some of the anxieties of the impelling death of the loved internalized and external objects—that is to say, in a lesser and milder degree the suffering and feelings that we find fully developed in the adult melancholic. Of course, these feelings are experienced in a different setting. The whole situation and the defences of the baby, which obtains reassurance over and over again in the love of the mother, differ greater from those in the adult melancholic. But the important point is that these sufferings, conflicts, and feelings of remorse and guilt, resulting actively from the relation of the ego to its internalized object, are already active in the baby. The same applies to paranoid and manic positions. If the infant at this period of life fails to establish its loved object within—if the introjection of the 'good' object miscarries—then the situation of the 'loss of the loved object' arises already in the same sense as it is found in the adult melancholic. This first and fundamental external loss of a real loved object, which is experienced through the loss of the breast before and during weaning, will only then result later on in a depressive state if at this early period of development the infant has failed to establish its loved object within its ego. It is also at this early stage of development that the manic fantasies, first controlling the breast and, very soon after, of controlling the internalized parents as well as the external ones, set in, with all the characteristics of the manic position. At any time that the child finds the breast again, after having lost it, the manic process by which the ego and ego-ideal to coincide (Freud) are going; for the child's gratification of being fed is not only felt to be a cannibalistic incorporation of external objects, however. The internalized loved objects and connects with the control over these objects. No doubt, the more the child can at this stage develop a happy relationship to its real mother, the more will it is able to overcome the depressive position. But all depends on how it is to find its way out of the conflict between love and uncontrollable hatred and sadism. In the realist phase the persecuting and good objects (breasts) are kept wide apart in the child's mind. When, along with the introjection of the whole and real object, they come closer together, the ego has over and over again recourse to that mechanism—so important for the development of the relations to objects—namely, a splitting of its imagoes into love and hatred, that is to say, into good and dangerous ones.

One might think that it is actually at this point that ambivalence that, after all, refers too object-relations—that is to say, to whole and real objects—sets in. Ambivalence, carries out in a splitting of the imagoes enabling the small child to gain more trust and belief in its real objects and thus in its internalized ones—to love them more and to carry out in an increasing degree its fantasies of restoration on the loved object. At the same time, the paranoid anxieties and defences are directed toward the 'bad' objects. The support that the ego gets from a real 'good' object is increased by a flight-mechanism, which alternates between its external and internal objects.

It seems that at this stage of development the unification of external and internal, loved and hated, real and imaginary objects are carried out in such a way that each step in the unification leads objects again, to a renewed splitting of the imagoes. But as the adaptation to the external world increases, this splitting is carried out on planes that gradually become increasingly nearer and nearer to reality. This goes on until love for the real and internalized objects and trust in them is well established. Then ambivalence, which is partly a safeguard against one's own hate and against the hatred and terrifying objects, will in normal development again diminish in varying degrees.

Along with the increase in love for one's good and real objects grows a greater trust in one's capacity to love and a lessening of the paranoid anxiety of the bad object—changes that lead to a decrease of sadism and again, to better ways of mastering aggression and working it off. The reparation-tendencies that play 'an all-important part in the normal process of overcoming the infantile depressive position are set going by different methods, of which two fundamental ones as that of the manic and the obsessional positions and mechanisms.

It would appear that the step from the introjection of part-objects to whole loved objects with all its implications is of the most crucial importance in development. Its success—it is true—depends largely on how the ego has been able to deal with its sadism and its anxiety in the preceding stage of development and whether or not it has developed a strong libidinal relation to part-objects. But once the ego has made this step it has, as it was, arrived at a crossroad from which the ways determining the whole mental make-up radiate in different directions.

Considerations about how a failure to maintain the identification with both internalized and real loved objects may result in the psychotic disorders of the depressive states, or of mania, or of paranoia.

There are, however, one or two other ways by which the ego attempts to make an end to all the suffering that are connected with the depressive position, namely: (a) By a 'flight of the good, internalized object,' a mechanism to which Melitta Schmideberg has drawn attention in connection with schizophrenia. The ego has introjected a whole loved object, but owing to its immoderate dread of internalized persecutors, which are projected onto the external world, the ego takes refuge in an extravagant belief in the benevolence of his internalized objects. The result of such a flight may be denial of psychic and external reality and the deepest psychosis.

By a flight to external 'good' objects as a means to disprove all anxieties—internal as well as external. This is a mechanism that is characteristic for neurosis and may lead to a slavish dependence on objects and a weakness of the ego.

These defence-mechanisms play their part in the normal working-through of the infantile depressive position. Failure to work successfully through this position may lead to the predominance of one or another of the flight-mechanisms referred to and thus to a severe psychosis or a neurosis.

# CHAPTER THREE

# Object Concept and Object Choice

It was in connection with Freud's revolutionary approach to the subject of sex and love that he developed the concept of the object. Expostulating the nature of the energy of the erotic drive, the libido, Freud (1905) distinguished between the zone of origin of the libido, the aim of the libidinal instinct, and the object of the instinct. It is upon the object that the libido is discharged and this process of discharge is experienced as pleasure. He said that the object was the mental representation of something that is the source of intense libidinal gratification, something highly cathected with the libido. The mental representation grows out of a mnemic image, a recollected set of sensory impressions accompanied by some pleasurable feeling tones that, according to the dominant principle one wishfully attempts to reconstitute a sensory impression that is part of one's person—the lips, skin, mouth, or anus, for example—or, it may be the mental representation of something inanimate which at a certain stage of cognitive development is still regarded as part of one's own person. Fenichel (1945) observed that a particular stage of the child's development, the faecal mass is viewed sometimes as part of the self and sometimes as part of the external world. This is a striking parallel to Winnicott's (1953) later concept of the transitional object. At a later stage the object may be a mental representation of something inanimate, of course, the object may be the mental representation of another person existing independently of the self. In each stage of this development, it should be emphasized, we are dealing with a technical term, the concept of a mental representation. According to libidinal theory, it is not the external thing that is vested with energy; it is the mental representation of the thing or person so cathected. The mental representation bears a special relationship to processes of instinctual discharge.

Emphasizing the representational aspect of the object highlights two kinds of confusion that pertains to the use of the object concept. The first of these confusions is illustrated by the theories of Wilhelm Reich (1942). Basing his views on Freud's earlier neurophysiological concepts, he regarded the libido as a material substance vested in some part of the self or in the body of another person. This approach has perpetuated the confusion between what is internal and what is external, that is, where in the physical world the material libido is to be found. It disregards the fact that at all times we are dealing with a psychological experience, the mental representation of an object, a persistently 'internal' experience.

The second confusion is illustrated by the concept of a part object as opposed to a whole object. Whatever it is that is represented mentally as instinctually cathected constitutes an object on mental representations of parts of one's own body, parts of someone else's body, or on mental representations of one's own or another person's whole body. Any one of these may be taken as an object. The type of unconscious fantasy involved determines whether or not the person's body is regarded as a penis or whether the person as a whole is regarded as a breast or, as in the case of narcissistic object choice, whether another person is regarded as a representation of one's own self. When we make judgements about psychological experiences, whether for the purpose of clinical interpretation or of theory building, what we try to determine is the nature of the unconscious fantasy that underlies the thought or behaviour of the individual, either in regard to other person's or things or in regard to the individual (Arlow, 1969). In such fantasies the mental representation of a breast may be fostered upon the image of a real external person or, conversely, one's whole body in an unconscious fantasy may be conceived as a representation of one's own or someone else's penis, breast, or faeces. In any event, we are dealing with mental representations of an object in the sense defined as the representation of one's own self, whether that mental representation corresponds to the totality of another person's body or to a part of one's own or another persons body.

A consequence of the confusion may be observed in the tendency to use the term interpersonal relations and object relations interchangeably. They are not identical. In fact, they represent two different realms of discourse. A young man, for example, disappointed in his beloved, does not search for a new object. He is really looking for another woman, who may in time become the source of pleasurable cathected mental representations. Fundamentally, it is the effect of unconscious fantasy wishes, connected with specific mental representations of objects, that colours, distorts, and affects the ultimate quality of interpersonal relations. It is important to distinguish between the person and the object. This is essentially, the core to transference, in which the person in the real world is confused with a mental representation of a childhood object, a mental representation of what one was either a person or a thing. These issues are not simply semantic ones. They bear directly on any discussions of love and narcissism and the role of object relations in ego development.

A few observations from the developmental point of view may place some of these problems in better focus. Psychoanalysis begins with the assumption that the pleasure principle is basic in all thee considerations. At birth the infant is little more than a passive reflexive animal. In his paper, 'The Primal Cavity,' Spitz (1955) described the conditions one may assume to pertain in the early sensorimotor or experience of the neonate. Perception of stimuli is registered in a global and indiscriminate fashion and, in keeping with inherently determined biological endowment, is felt as either pleasurable or unpleasurable. These sensorimotor experiences leave memory traces in the developing psyche. Only gradual does the infants begin to distinguish between different types of sensory experiences and leaves to assign the stimuli to their proper sources of local and origin. A signal turning point is reached when a judgement can be made on whether the stimulus arises within the body or outside of it. The experiential and cognitive processes that make this advance possible have been descried and detailed by many authors.

According to Freud (1911), the operation of the pleasure principle is expressed through a tendency to reestablish and experience a set of sensory perceptions of a pleasurable nature identical with the memory of earlier experiences of pleasure. Thus, the first and fundamental categorization of experience is in terms os pleasure or in terms of pleasant or unpleasant. (Brenner [1974], in his study of the development of affects, has demonstrated the fundamental structures.) This is the abiding principle by which perceptions are integrated and organized in memory according to the quality of similarity with or differences from earlier memory traces. On the basis of how the memory of earlier perceptions has been organized, subsequent experiences tend to be grouped together, depending upon whether they are associated or connected with memories of pleasurable or unpleasurable affects.

In the earliest phases the organization of the object concept is under the protection of the pleasure principle. What is pleasurable is at first treated as part of the self, and in keeping with pleasure principle, the psychic apparatus operated toward trying to institute a repetition of the perceptions. It is not hard to understand how reality testing and the interpretation of sensory data, function acquired with such effort, are easily and readily set aside in the compulsive wishful striving of dreams, fantasies, and neurotic symptoms, as well as under the influence of great passion or prejudice, and, of course, in love. The fundamental tendency to seek an identity of pleasurable perceptions goes far in explaining the persistent influence of unconscious childhood fantasies.

What is later organized and conceptualized as the need-gratifying object originates out of the memories of repetitive sensory impressions accompanied by feelings of gratification. Object seeking is predominantly oriented by the need to try to achieve the identity of pleasurable perceptions remembered but not too attainable by infants. The disparity between infants' wishes and their limited capacity to achieve them in reality is a fundamental fact of human development. Subsequently the memory traces of pleasurable sensory impression connected with an external person become organized into a coherent memory structure, a mental representations of a person, which we call 'object.' The term, object, therefore, represents a concept concerning a persistent, that is, a structured experience. In parallel fashion in a coherent organization of memory traces of representations connected with pain may serve as the basis for the concept of another kind of an object representation. Thus it happens that two sets of memories of sensory impressions may be organized as mental representations, one associated with pain, the other with pleasure. The pleasant representations of such memories may be labelled as good and the unpleasant ones as bad. It is in this sense that is to be understood in what the Kleinians mean when they talk about 'good' objects and 'bad' objects in referring to the psychic events in the earliest months of life.

It is only later in the course of development that the seemingly disparate mental representations of objects having identical sensory impressions are fused into the concept of an external person whose mental representations psychologically may be vested or associated with memories of pain as well as pleasure. From a psychological point of view the individual's concept of a person is a conglomeration of many earlier object representations. This coherent, organized concept may be dissolved regressively into an antecedent object representation. It is in this sense that it can be called the theory of 'splitting.' It is not necessarily the re-emergence of an earlier structure, but rather the reactivation of memory traces of a bad object representation, thus, the splitting of the representation of a person does not necessarily occur. Only in cases of severe personality regression. When there is a painful interaction between two people, one can observe in the dreams and fantasies of the patient how the qualities of good and bad may become sharply dissociated in the mental representations of the object. The individual, in turn, may respond to the other person as if that person were the repetition of the earlier mental representation of the bad object. At the same time, such an individual may be functioning at an advanced level of mental development. The case with which the coherent concept of the object may regressively dissolve into earlier disparate mental representations is a measure of ego weakness. The tendency to split the object representations into 'good' and 'bad' antecedent expression is usually reversible. In severe pathology, however, the process is irreversible and the split of the object representation becomes fixed and persistent.

Mahler's (1975) concepts of separation-individuation are well known, and the observational base for these concepts has been well established. Her ideas are frequently invoked to explain certain phenomena's observed in the borderline states, the psychoses, falling in love, and the experience of the orgasm. The stages before the phases of separation-individuation have been associated with the period of primary identification—the stage during which there is no differentiation between the self and that of the object. Regression to primary identification is a hypotheses that have in appeal to those who view a good segment of psychopathology reflecting a 'loss of boundaries' between the self and the object. According to some, this is the condition that regressively reactivates in the psychopathological formation, however, it should be noted that feeling at one with everything being completely identified with someone, thinking that someone experiences and feels everything that another person seems to feel, is necessarily a recapitulation of the vague, undefined states that precede the distinction between the self and that of the object world. When poets describe the ecstasy of love or orgasm by saying that they feel completely united and indissolvably fused with the beloved, there is nonetheless, some concomitant awareness of the existence of the other person as an independent object. This is equally true for descriptions of timelessness and so-called 'oceanic' feeling, two states of mind often associated with being in love as well as with loss of the sense of self of or 'ego boundaries.' In a study of distortions of the sense of time (Arlow, 1974), as how the sensation of timelessness actually represented derivatives of an unconscious fantasy. When analyzed, the unconscious fantasy was not that of the fusion of self and object. In one instance, the fantasy expresses a woman's wish to have her oedipal love object forever. In the case of a male patient, it represented an overcoming of the fear of castration, a wish for immortality to counteract the pressing awareness of the danger of castration as represented by a fear of death.

Freud (1914) in his work titled 'On Narcissism,' emphasized that in severe, regressive narcissistic disorders, there is not only a break with reality and withdrawal from objects on the external world, but at the same time, one is unable to find any trace of cathexis of mental representations of objects in fantasy, conscious or unconscious. It should be emphasized that it is not the clinical phenomenon of isolation withdrawal from people that indicate a break of object relations, but the evidence of withdrawal of cathexis from mental representation of objects. This is an important distinction to bear in mind; otherwise one is tempted to make extrapolations from phenomenology without appreciating the characteristic feature of psychoanalysis, namely, the nature of the unconscious psychological experience. It is possible for certain individuals to have very poor relations with people, but at the same time maintaining a very high quality of object constancy in fantasy life. One has to avoid judging the significance of an experience by externally observable phenomena alone.

In at least, a beginning attempt at individuation and after the phase of the transitional object, the different constellations of the memories of sensory experiences of pleasure and pain may be organized around the common source of perceptions into the concept of the good and bad mother, the good and bad object. One aspect of the child's growing ability to master ambivalence resides in the capacity to integrate the two contradictory concepts into a specific, unified concept of a person in the external world. Developmental psychologists, different as to exactly when this achievement is attained—probably sometime in the second year of life. It is an attainment, however, that is easily and regularly undone by regression. The concept of the object, as well as the concept of the self and even of the Superego may undergo regressive dissolution into their antecedent identifications. This may be observed in dreams and in psychopathology, especially in patient's suffering from depression, both in the borderline states and in the psychoses.

A few observations about the Superego will serve to illustrate these ideas. The Superego is not a unified agency closely observed, it can be seen to constitute an organization of contradictory trends based upon an attempt to integrate various impressions of experiences of judging and of having been judged, of reward and punishment from objects. This agency of the mind is built up, for the most part by way of identification with objects in very specific contexts. The self-condemning, persecutor, hallucinations observed in various forms of severe depression represent memories or fantasies, distorted, it is true, by the process of defence, but memories that have been regressively transformed into visual or auditory perceptions. Under such circumstances, the delusional material regressively recapitulates, by way of identification. The process reveals that the identifications in the Superego, in terms of the individual'S previous conflicts.

These considerations are important because identification plays a major role in object relations theory, especially as applied to love. Identification, like object relations, cannot be separated from drive derivatives. The two concepts are indissolvably linked in experience. Identification is implicit in the concept of internalized object relations, but such object relations are part of a continuum of drive discharge. An identification is not effected with the totality of another person or object but with some specific aspects of the person's behaviour are selected for purposes of identification are congruent with or corresponds to certain drive needs of the individual. These may relate primarily to id fulfilment of wishes, to ego's purpose of defences, or to Superego efforts directed toward self-punishment.

In the spirit of the conclusions reached by Altman (1977) we can repeat that there is no clear delineation of any specific syndrome that we call loving or being in love. Putting aside for the moment the social influences and the educational processes that structure and present models for individual behaviour, we realize that we are dealing essentially with different patterns of object choice. We are struck by the dramatic, compulsive quality with which certain, but, by no means all, individual's pursue the object. Does such pursuit differ in any fundamental way from other repetitive, seemingly compulsive, uncontrollable, unstable compromise formation effected by the three psychic agencies in other normal and pathological processes—for example, symptom formation, dreams, perverse impulses? The varieties of psychopathological formation. As well as the varieties of normal compromising reaction. From this point of view it is difficult to agree completely with Bak (1973), who tried to trace the psychology of loving to a specific developmental vicissitude, the wish to re-achieve symbiotic fusion with the mother in order to undo the primordial separation. This early vicissitude of object relations must have some bearing on the patterns of loving, but while it is not necessarily decisive.

The great diversity of patterns of loving can be illustrated from the experience in any analyst's practice. There is a rich literature ranging from Freud's studies in the psychology of love to the more recent discussions of self-object narcissistic choice. Freud's (1917) 'Taboo of Virginity,' is important in one special way, inasmuch as, to illustrate the role of aggression in the choice of the love object and in the pattern of loving. The same principles apply to object choice made in certain of the sexual perversions. But the truly complex nature of the patterns of loving and object choice can best be represented by the study of individual patients.

In anyone individual it is possible to observe different patterns of loving and varieties of object choices. Take, for example, the typical oedipal evolution of the patient traumatized by the primal scene who develops a persistent unconscious rescue fantasy together with a need for a degraded love object. A concomitant persistent wish may be to wreak vengeance upon surrogates for the betraying, unfaithful mother. Furthermore, in response to the fear of castration generated by the anticipation of retaliation for hostile wishes against the father, the same individual may develop a pattern of passive, submissive, feminine orientations toward men. In such a patient can be such as in the variety of patterns of loving and object choices toward members of both sexes, characterized by patterns of instinctual gratification that represent both aim-inhibited and aim-fulfilled wishes. In derivative of several types of unconscious fantasies, representing wishes derived from different moments in his relations to the important wishes derived from different types representing wishes derived from different moments in his relation to the important objects of his past, the patient identified himself with different objects as his father, his mother, the crucified Christ, certain figures from mythology and fairy-tails. Each identification found expression in some form of loving. The identifications were the vehicle for drive derivatives, part of an unconscious fantasy of being either the father, the father's sexual partner, or some heroic conqueror. His patterns of loving relations with both men and women were determined by the nature of the persistent unconscious fantasies. Loving involves identification, but identification at many levels and at many different times with different objects. It is not necessarily a regressive reactivation of the primitive fusion with a love object or regression to a phase where there is no distinction between the self and the object world.

With the analytic situation closer examination of the phenomenon of love demonstrates how certain aspects of the real person and of the self are rigorously excluded in the sense of oneness. What is experienced is determined by a fantasy or a set of wishes centring about mental representations deriving from selected memories of experiences with the earlier object or objects—the father, the mother, and in the unusual cases, oneself or parts of one's body.

By way of comparison, one may observe another patient, in whom there were several distinct patterns of love relations. He was, first of all, a very successful Don Juan who typically won, seduced, and then abruptly dropped his partner. The abruptness with which he ends these relationships was parallelled by the urgent intensity with which he pursued them in the beginning. If one concentrated only on the opening phases of his relationships, he would seem to epitomize the romantic ideal of his relationships, he would seem to epitomize the romantic ideal of the love-intoxicate, heartsick young swain. In these affairs, however, the culmination of the relationship was represented not by the successful libidinal gratification, but rather by the gratification of aggression directed toward the woman. The original object in this was not the promiscuous, disappointing oedipal and post-oedipal mother, but also an abandoning nursemaid who had abruptly left the family's employment when the patient was three and a half year's of age.

In contrast, the same patient also had long-lasting, devoted sexual attachments to older women, relationships that were regularly stormy, but compulsively maintained, remarkably ambivalent, and characterized by vehement mutual recriminations. These relationships recapitulated a clandestine affair he had, had with a housekeeper-nursemaid, an affair that lasted through the oedipal and latency periods and parallelled in time the disillusioning experiences with his mother. The patient's love relations with older women were sadomasochistic in quality and articulate specific forms of anal-erotic gratification that could be traced to the character of the housekeeper-nursemaid. Residue attachments could be seen in the aim-inhibited love relationship he had with his secretary, a much older woman, as well as in the nature of his own character structure, which reflected an identification with the clandestine lover through the compulsive anal behaviour he pursued identification with her. The active, phallic nature of this woman undoubtedly predisposed the patient to make subsequent oedipal and post-oedipal object choices of women who were active and sensual and whose behaviour corresponded to his fantasy of the woman possessing a penis. The Dion Juan behaviour was multiplied determined, a mixture of the fulfilment of erotic and aggressive impulses, and identification with the faithless, promiscuous mother, the abandoning love object, together with elements of defence against castration anxiety. While much more could be said about the determinants of the specific and complex pattern of loving in this case, it clearly illustrates the complicating interrelationship of identification, defence, object relations, and instinctual gratification, all of which play a role in determining the nature of the patient's love. It would be impossible to reduce the plexuities of object-finding and gratification to any of the simple basic formulas proposed by several of the proponents of object relations theory.

The subject of identification quite naturally leads to the topic of internalized object relations. This is a concept that is very difficult to differentiate from identification. Does it mean more than the fact that the personality or psychic structure of an individual is transformed as the result of his or her interaction with others? Or, does internalized object relation imply the positing of a persistent structure in the psychic apparatuses which has a dynamic thrust of its own, a thrust to repeat and reproduce the original experience in a way that is independent of the drive representation? Is there a developmental thrust which asserts itself along predetermined lines through a hierarchical distinction to stages, beginning with the earliest relations and progressing toward an ideal end-point commonly known as the mature or genital form of object relationships, which presumably leads to the 'highest' stage of love? In discussions of internalized object relations theory and love, it seems that this developmental eventuality is considered as the 'sine quoi non' of true love.

It would seem that, nonetheless, in the elements of value judgements infiltrate analytic considerations of love. This is a trend which can be traced to the early history of psychoanalysis. It is difficult to avoid a tendency to judge psychological phenomena in terms that essentially means 'good' or 'bad.' Some such tendencies may be discerned in Abraham's (1924) study of the development in terms of biology. The quality of the libidinal tie with any individual, Abraham maintained, is determined by the level of psychosexual development which it reflects. The development of sexuality evolved in precise stages and subdivisions by way of a normal, orderly succession of dominance by oral, anal, and phallic instinctual drives. The nature of the object chosen was determined by the dive dominant at the particular stage when the choice was made. The highest stage of development, the mature form of love, was genital love. By way of contrast, choices effected at the pregenital level, Abraham considered preambivalent or ambivalent, a quality which poor prognostic outcome, because it conveyed the potentiality for conflict and neurosogenesis. Genital love, in its postambivalent form, typifies those qualities which society regards as both desirable and commendable in the relationship between two people of the opposite sex. To be sure, these qualities have unquestioned social unity insofar as they strengthen the ties which make for a stable marriage and foster the solidarity of the family, the basic unit of society. From society's point of view, an ideal postambivalent genital relationship is desirable, useful, and therefore 'good.'

Today, more than half a century later, the terminology and leading conceptualizations may have changed, but the problem remains the same. Formulations are now couched in terms of object relations instead of biology; the distinctions between the self and the object world have become the touchstones. Instead of an orderly, biological predetermined succession of libidinal stages, what is emphasized today is the developmental evolution of an orderly set of stages of object relations.

According to Friedman (1978), this process is considered by many to be equally predetermined as an inexorable developmental thrust, much in the same spirit as Abraham's formulation concerning libidinal phases and the concomitant object choices. While Abraham emphasized the developmental aspects of libidinal drive over the nature and vicissitudes of experience with the object, more recent formulations in terms of object relations theory tended to emphasize the vicissitudes of experience with the object, as well as the resultant cognitive and affective consequences. Thus, certain authors maintain that true love is possible only in the context of mature object relations, that the capacity to love truly implies that the individual's object relations have progressed to the highest level of development.

We have a dilemma. One contributor to the psychology of love from the point of view of object relations maintains that love represents a re-emergence of the earliest, most primitive mother-child relationship, while another asserts that love reflects the most developed, most mature form of object relations.

A hierarchy of stages of object relations culminating in a so-called 'mature' relationship is essentially an idealized concept. Clinical experience underscores the fact that in every love relationship the individual acts out some form of complicated unconscious fantasy rooted in early vicissitudes of drive and object experience, a fantasy that ultimately determines, but only in part, the pattern of loving and the specific person or types of persons that will correspond to the object choice. Bergmann (1980) notes that one of his patient's, commenting on his love relations, stated that he was playing out a scenario for his love affair. While he was conscious of only one scenario, at the same time there was another, an unconscious scenario that was being played out without the patient being aware of it. This is probably true of all patients in their love relation, as well as in other object ties. Accordingly, to the extent that something from the infantile past forms parts of every love relationship, the concept of a mature object relationship in love is something of an idealization and contrary to what one encounters in actual analytic practice. In many respects, what Freud (1911) said about fantasy in the world of reality may be said about love relationships, he compared fantasy to its nature of preservation, somewhat like Algonquin Provincial Park—a bit of the pristine wilderness preserved within the confines of civilization.

Even in so-called mature object relations love, there are many recognizable infantile remnants, and they are by no means all pathological. The loving relationship is a bit of unreality set aside from the world of reality. Many aspects of the relationship between lovers clearly reflect infantile prototypes of behaviour—for instance, baby talk. Nor does it follow that an object choice based upon an infantile wish necessarily dooms the love to failure or even to instability. Unions based on an oedipal rescue fantasy need not spell catastrophe, if there is some element of congruence or complementarity in the mutual choice of objects. Eisentein (1956) collected many such examples in his book, 'Neurotic Interaction in Marriage.' One of the striking examples in that book was Jacobson (1956) who described the nature of the object ties which brought together psychotic personalities in a lasting relationship. Such ties do not always involve the element of mutual identification based upon similar unconscious fantasy wishes.

Love relations integrate complex needs of individuals who come together in keeping with conditions operative at various phases of their lives. These needs may change in time for many reasons, altering the relationships between the partners, and this is what leads to instability or rupture of the relationship or to the search for new love. In finding a new object, the individual may or may not repeat the old pattern. To a large extent what happens is determined by the nature of the unconscious conflict which the individual is trying to resolve at that particular time in life. A classic example of this may be seen in Freud's (1917), 'Taboo of Virginity.' There he describes certain women who experience defloration as castration. As a result, they hold a grudging, vengeful attachment to their first lovers, tied to them ion a thralldom of hostility. If they marry the first lover, the marriage is usually doomed to failure. A second marriage, however, may turn out quite well. This clinical observation by Freud should caution us against a rigid, one-sided application to the object relations aspect to specific difficulties of loving.

From the developmental point of view, one must be cautious in trying to predict the nature of later object ties and patterns of loving on the basis early experiences with the object ties. For example, in a study upon the observing inactions between the mother and child in the nursery from the point of view of how in character of the child was transformed. They could not predict what aspects of the object the child would choose as the basis for identification, nor could they delineate retrospectively why certain identifications had in fact been effected. In other words, it is not just the experience with the object, but what is done with the experience, that is decisive for development, this has some bearing on the development of the capacity to love. Later experiences in love relationships may modify the effect of earlier object ties (Beres and Obers, 1950).

Love is an affective state, and in all affective states the patterning of the outward expression of inner feelings is in large measure determined by culture. In our daily work with patients, we are constantly passing judgement on whether the patient's effective response is in keeping with, i.e., appropriate to; his or her experience. We make such judgements in terms of standards relevant to our culture and to the individuals background. Cultural influences not only how love is expressed, but also how it is experienced. The cultural influence may be transcended the specific set of interactions as characterized by their characteristic relation with the infantile object in evolving the fusion of the tender and the impulse of the libidinal forces. Object as a notion that was canonized during the romantic period. It is not always the model for the choice of a partner; and even today it represents a notion as of an honoured breach as in the observance to that of other times and other levels of society, having, in fact, institutionalized the distinction between these various components of what we call 'being in love,' they have done so by the institution its marriage customs, property arrangements, and sanctioned extra marital liaisons. There have been and still are many polygamous societies. The significance of institutionalized practices of predominant social patterns for courtship and for choosing a mate can hardly be lost on the younger members of any society. 'Love at first sight,' 'falling head over heels in love,' 'loving in despair, from afar,' 'the attraction of the unattainable object,' all represent styles of experiencing and expressing love. They are styles that have their ascendancy and decline. In yesteryears, the idealization of the love object and its public expression were encouraged by social norms.

As analysts, we pass judgement on the phenomenology of love we observe in our patients. We do so in terms of phase-specific anticipations. For example, we accept but hardly ever really analyzed reports of impulsive patterns of loving that patients present concerning their adolescence. We relate this to the clearly present physiological transformations of puberty. On the other hand, we may look as showing disapproval at thee middle-aged man, and certainly at an elderly man, who falls in love following the adolescent pattern. In the same spirit, one has to note the social bias against older women having liaisons with younger men; the reverse pattern is more acceptable. These are subtle but definitive value judgements as couched in terms of normal, that is, statistically anticipated. Unconsciously, they dictate to us what and how we choose to analyse.

In actual practice we are concerned with what has led to a particular patient to love in her or his particular way; how, among the myriad patterns of love, the patient has come to select the one he or she actually did choose. How well we are able to determine this depends in large measure upon how close the distance is between the choice of object and the pattern of loving, and the central nexus of the patient's unconscious conflict's. The consequences of conflict make it possible for us to analyse the nature of the love relationship; but in those instances in which the pattern of loving is ego-syntonic, we have less of an opportunity to penetrate deeply into the psychology of love and are therefore not in a very good position to grasp some understanding of the precursors of the particular patterns of loving. Under such circumstances, the temptation is great to interpret and to speculate phenomenologically rather than dynamically. What we do, in effect is conjecture on the basis of history about what might have been the individual's psychological experience, since we seem unable to trace out the interpretation inferentially from the data supplied in the dynamic context of the analytic situation.

## REFERENCES

- Abraham K. (1924): A Short Study of the Development of the Libido Viewed in the Light of Mental Disorders. In. Selected Papers on Psychoanalysis. New York: Basic Books, Inc., 1953: pp. 418-501.
- Altman; J. A. (1977): Some Vicissitudes of Love: E. J. Amer. Press. Assn., XXV. pp. 35-52.
- Arlow, J. A. (1969): Unconscious Fantasy and Disturbances of Conscious Experience-(1974): Disturbances of the Sense of Time. Freud Memorial Lectures. New York. Psychoanalytic Institute, April 16.
  -(1979): Metaphor and the psychoanalytic Situation. Psychoanal. Quarterly, XXVIII, pp. 363-385.
- Bak, R. (1973): Being in Love and Object Loss. Int. J. Psa., LIV, pp 1-8.
- Beres, D. And Obers, S. J. (1950): The Study of Ego Development t. In the Psychoanalytic Study of the Child. Vol. V. New York International Universities Press, Inc., pp. 212-235.
- Bergmann, M. S. (1971): Psychoanalytic Observations on the Capacity to Love. In: Separation-Individuation ; Essays in Honour of Margaret S. Mahler, Edited by J. McDevitt and C. Settlage. New York: International Universities Press, Inc., pp. 15-40.
  -(1980): On the Intrapsychic Function of Falling in Love. Psychoanal. Quarterly, XLIX. pp. 56-77.
- Boesky, C. (1980): Introduction to Symposium on Object Relations Theory and Love: Psychoanal. Quarterly, XLIII. pp. 48-55.
- Brenner, C. (1974): On the Nature of Development of Affects: A Unified Theory. Psychoanal. Quarterly,. XLIX. Pp. 532-556.
- Eisenstein, C., Editor (1956): Neurotic Interaction in Marriage. New York: Basic Books, Inc.
- Fenichel, O. (1945): The Psychoanalytic Theory of Neurosis. New York: W. W. Norton & Co.
- Freud (1905): Three Essays on the Theory of Sexuality. Standard Edition, VII. Pp. 135-243.
  -(1911); Formulations on the Two Principles of Mental Functioning. Standard Edition, XII. Pp. 218-226,
  -(1914): On Narcissism: An Introduction. Standard Edition, XIV, pp. XIV, pp. 73-102.
  -(1917): The Taboo of Virginity. Standard Edition, XI. Pp. 193-208.
  -(1925) (Negation). Standard Edition. XIX, pp. 235-239.

* Friedman, L. (1978):Trends in Psychoanalytic Theory of Treatment. Psychoanal. Quarterly, XLVII, Inc., pp. 125-134.
* Jacobson, E. (1956): Interaction between Psychotic Partners, In:. Manic-Depressive Partners, In: Neurotic Interaction in Marriage. Edited by V. Eisenstein. New York: Basic Books, Inc., pp. 740-763.
* Mahler, M. S. (1967):On Human Symbiosis and Vicissitudes of Individuation. J. Amer Psa. Assn., XV, pp. 740-763.
  -Pine, F. Bergman, A. (1975): The Psychological Birth of the Human Infant. Symbiosis and Individuation. New York. Basic Books, Inc.
* Reich, Wilhelm (1942): The Function of the Orgasm. (The Discovery of the Orgasm, Vol. I.) New York: Orgone Institute Press.
* Ritvo S. And Solnit A. (1958): influences of Early Mother-Child Interaction on identification Processes. In: The Psychoanalytic Study of the Child, Vol. XIII. New York: International Universities Press. Inc., pp. 215-240.
* Spitz, R. (1955):The Primal Cavity. In`The Psychoanalytic Study of the Child, Vol. X New York: International Universities Press, Inc., pp. 215-240.
* Winnicott, D. W. (1953): Transitional Objects and Transitional Phenomena: A Study of the First Not-Me Possession. Inc. J. Psa., XXXIV., pp. 89-97.

# CHAPTER FOUR

# Object Relationships and Affects

THE DEVELOPMENT OF OBJECT relationships, with special reference to the role of affect in the development, is not a topic so easily to discuss because the psychoanalytic theory is far from satisfactory, and our theory of affect is, at best, in a state of healthy and constructive chaos. When we think about object relationships we have to cope in our minds with such concepts as relationships which possess object-constancy. We have objects to whom there is an anaclitic relationship toward whom we are ambivalent, who are narcissistic objects, self objects, or simply good or bad objects. There are objects with whom we have sadomasochistic relationships, objects biological and objects psychological and many others. In the face of all this we have found it increasingly necessary to ask ourselves how the theory of object relationships can be integrated into our intrapsychic psychoanalytic psychology.

It was certainly appropriate, for some considerable time during the development of psychoanalytic theory, to regard an object relationship as the 'cathexis of an object' with libidinal or aggressive energy. This is a way of saying that within the energid frame of reference, that an object relationship is the state of loving, or of both loving and hating, another person or and aspect of that person. But it is increasingly clear that conceiving of an object relationship as the energid investment of an object is inadequate and simplistic (Joffe and Sandler, 1967). We know, for example, that object relationships are two-sided, that they equally involve activity on the part of the other person (for example, the care taking mother). We also know that our thoughts and feelings about the important objects in our lives, our behaviour toward them and our expectations from them are extremely complex. This begins with the intricate interaction between the child and his biological objects in the earliest weeks and months of life. Phenomena such as these have been studied outside the treatment situation by psychoanalytic child observers such as Ren Spitz (e.g., 1959, 1965), Donald Winnocott (e.g., 1953, 1960, 1971), Margaret Mahler and her colleagues (Mahler, 1975). Bowlby (1969, 1973), as well by many experimenters working in a systematic way was more recently on the reaction of very young infants to the different people in their environment (Stone, 1974; Rexford, 1976). On the basis of theoretical reconstructions from analytic material, some analysts (notably, Melanie Klein and her followers) have stressed the plexuity of early object relationships (Klein, 1932, 1957; Isaac, 1948).

The relationship between two people, even if looked at from only one side in terms of the subjective experience and activities of one of the people concerned, involves very subtle and complicated cues and signs. There are unconscious exchanges of messages, as well as the conscious or unconscious experiencing of all sorts of other interactions. Each partner, at any given moment, has a role for the other, and negotiates with the other to get him or her to respond in a particular way. A whole variety of feelings, wishes, thoughts and expectations are involved in the interaction which is characteristic of the ongoing relationship between two people. This is not only true for a relationship between two people, an object relationship fantasy will also involve a similar sort of interaction between self and object representations, except that in fantasy relationship the person having the fantasy can control the fantasy relationship in a wish-fulfilling way to a much greater degree than he can in real life.

The question of wish-fulfilment and gratification is extremely important in regard to object relationships. Wherefore, we can assume that what we call object relationships, and, in so doing, representing the fulfilment of important needs, developing as the child as well as in the adolescent and adult. Such needs—in a sense of role relationships, needs not are predominant. It is a common error to equate the general concept of the unconscious wish with the particular case of mental apparatus which is unconscious in the descriptive sense, but which is not id. Many wishes arise within the mind as responses to motivating forces which are not instinctual. Perhaps the commonest of such motivators are anxieties and other unpleasant affects, but we must equally include the effect of disturbances of inner equilibrium created by stimuli from the outside world, as motivators of need and psychological wishes. The wishes which are aroused may be conscious, but may not be, and very importantly are not, they may have a drive component, or a developmental relation to the instinctual drives, but this is not a necessary course of ingredient of an unconscious wish, this is not necessary current ingredient to an unconscious wish. Such a such wish, fore example, be simply to remove in a particular way whatever is (conscious or unconsciousness) identification as a source of discomfort, pain, or unpleasure. The wish may be (and is often) motivated by the need to restore feelings of well-being and safety, or may be connected with anyone normally called 'instinctual'. Wishes are aroused by 'change' in the object world as much as by internal pressures.

We have spoken of the various needs of the individual, instinctual and otherwise (including all those which arise from disturbances of this internal equilibrium) and the wishes which develop in associations with these needs. To this we have to add something extremely important. The individual is constantly obtaining a special form of gratification through his interaction with his environment and with his own self something which in the object relationship we can refer to as 'affirmation.' Through his interaction with different aspects of his world, in particular his objects, he gains a variety of reassuring feelings. We put forward the thesis that the need for this 'nourishment,' for affirmation and reassurance, has to be satisfied constantly in order to yield a background of safety. We usually see such needs only when their ongoing toddlers who play happily while mother is at her corner of the room, only occasionally glancing at her, or running to her from time to time, who can continue their play because of the constant interchanging of signals with the mother, an interchange which provides a feeling of security with the mother, and interchange which provide a feeling of security and well-being. If, however, such a toddler notices that his mother has left the room, a need to perceive her to interact with her, to hold on to her, will immediately become apparent. This will express itself in the form of a very intense wish with a very infinite content, we can see that this sort of object relationship is certainly very much a continual wish-fulfilment, in which the wish is to obtain reassurance that the mother is nearby (thus fulfilling the need to feel safe). Later in life, the child (and adult) will increasingly be able to make use of an unconscious dialogue with hi s objects in fantasy in order maintain in reassurance.

It should be noted that, in the follows, affects will be looked at entirely from the point in feeling within aa may be, the pleasurable and outside in the unpleasable such free-states may be within the conscious awakeners as stated elsewhere by Sandler, 1974.

If we can allow ourselves to depart from the widely held (but mistaken) view that all unconscious wishes are motivated solely by instinctual drives we can then concede that (just like the need for pleasure)—for example, a wish to run away in order escape an external danger situation. However, although at one time such wishes my be acceptable to us, during development they my become unacceptable, and remain as urgent but unconscious wishful impulses and remain as urgent but unconscious wishful impulses which are defended against. Wishes which represent past solutions and other factors, particularly childhood ones, constantly recur but may be kept back because they are no longer acceptable in the present, with new ones to re-experience important subjective aspects of object relationships, from the first years of life constantly recur and persists of security or safety are threatened as they constantly are. One of the main aims of the mental apparatus can be said to be that of protecting consciousness. As a consequent, the way in which we gratify or fulfil unconscious wishes of all sorts may be extremely subtle and disguised, because of the needs to protect consciousness.

Thus we may repeat the past object relationships embodied in an unconscious wish in a disguised form. Although our behaviour does not, of course, consist only in repeating past object relations. It is certainly true that a great deal of our life is involved in the concealed reception of early object relations in one form or another. This includes those patterns of relationship which have developed as safety-giving or anxiety-deducing manoeuvrers, as well as those which satisfy instinctual wishes. Which of what we call illness, including occasionally quite severe psychological illness, may be looked at from this point of view. And, it need hardly be added, all the defensive displacements, reversals, and other forms of disguise, can enter into the way in which we repeat or attempt to repeat wish-fulfilment in early relationship.

In psychological terms, every wish involved a self representation, object representation, and representation of the interaction between these. There is a role for both self and object. Thus, for example, the child who has a wish to cling to the mother, has, as part of this wish a mental representation of himself clinging to the mother. But he also has, in that content of his wish, a representation of the mother or her substitute responding to his clinging in a particular way, possibly by bending down and embracing him. This formulation is rather different from the idea of a wish consisting of a wishful aim being directed toward an object. The idea of an aim which seeks gratification has to be supplemented by the idea of a wish-for interaction, with the wished-for imagined responses of the object being as much apart of a wishful fantasy as the activity of the subject in that wish or fantasy.

All of this relates to the clinical topic of transference and countertransference relevant aspects of which have been discussed elsewhere (J. Sandler, 1976). The idea of transference need not be restricted to the way in which the patient distorts his perception of the analyst, but can be taken to include all the unconscious and often very subtle attempts by the patient to manipulate the analyst in the psychoanalytical situation in order to evoke a particular type of response in him (Sandler, 1973). Transference can be said to include the attempt to bring about a situation which would be a disguised repetition of an earlier experience or relationship, or be defence against the repetition of such relationship. The person manipulated in this way outside the analysis may reject or ignore the role, or alternative may be accepted. To, or in part of it, was felt that the unconscious acceptance or rejection of a role was based on a series of rapid unconscious cues given and taken in the interchange between two people. While transference elements are present to some degree in all relationships, what is also necessary for a real relationship of any significance to be established in the propensity of the second person, toward whom the transference is directed, to react in a special way, and in the process of object-choice he is subtly tested to see whether he will respond in a particular way or not. This reflects what has been called his 'role-responsiveness' (J. Sandler, 1976). The idea of 'testing out' of another person brings together the concept of object choice and object relationship, inasmuch as we make rapid relationships until we find someone who fits the role we want the 'other' to play and is prepared to allow himself to respond according to that role. What had been previously formulated in this connexion for transference (Sandler, 1973) can be seen to be an important part of object relationships overall.

Not only do the concepts of object choice and object relationship come together if we think in terms of the individual seeking particular role relationships (in the transference, or outside it in his everyday life) but the traditional distinction between the search for objects on the one hand and the search for wish-fulfilment or need-satisfaction on the other, fading into insignificance. The two can be regarded for being essentially the same. If a person creates stable object relationships, then he creates through his interaction with his objects, through their mutual effectively significant communication, both a constantly recurring source of wish-fulfilment and a constant object relationship.

Our clinical experience brings it home to us that in object relatively may have a very definite pattern, a time sequence, inherent on it. We all know of cases in which someone gets on well with an employee or a lover, and after a certain number of weeks or months a sudden disappointment or disillusionment occurs. In analysis this can often be traced either to an adaptive pattern of relationship from childhood to a defence against dangerous closeness. What is important is that the relationship has a temporal dimension. There is a script for dialogue.

It could be said that the patient in analysis attempts to actualize the particular role relationship, inherent in his current dominant unconscious. Wishes or fantasy, and that he will try to do this (usually in a disguising and symbolic way) within the framework of the psychoanalytic situation. People also do this outside analysis, and it is not a great step to say that the striving toward actualization is part of the wish-fulfilling aspect of all object relationships. The term 'actualization' is used in the dictionary sense and not of the special technical senses in which it is used by a number of author. It is simply 'a making actual,' a 'realization in action of fact' and discussing this topic elsewhere (J. Sandler, 1976) it has been pointed out that the analysis does not only make use of his free-floating attention, but also has what can be called a free-floating responsiveness to the patient and will often to a certain degree, allow himself to do. Some analysis will have wider limitation in one case than another, or may even comply completely with the role with unconsciously demanded to them. When this happens in the analyst and will often see himself behaving (or, feel tempted to behave) in an apparent irrational way, which he in fact responded through his self analysis to be apparently neurotic; and through his self analysis to be apparently neurotic; and yet, he has, in a sense, 'pressed the right buttons in him.' Although the analysis certainly has propensity of his own to function in a way, his reaction may represent his compliance with the role that the patient wants him to play. Sometimes we only get the useful information which this can provide after we have, for example, notices a departure from our usual way of dealing with the patient. These enactments, or role-evocations, can provide useful information to the analyst about the wish-fulfilling object relationship which the patient is unconsciously trying to actualize in the transference. Of course, not all irrational behaviour on the part of the analyst should be regarded as a role-response to the patient, but much of this is.

In the previous study the view was put forward that wish-fulfilment overall occurs through actualization of one sort or another (Sandler, 1976). This was studied in relation to dreams in particular, where we unconsciously obtain wish-fulfilment through hallucinatory actualization, with conscious being 'deceived' about what is occurring. It was postulated that there is also an 'understanding work' which parallels the dream work, as described by Freud. This understanding work is part of the perception of the dream. So that the dream content is unconsciously understood a wish-fulfilment, about what is occurring consciously and must be protected at all times and at all costs by the description of the dream work, but an essential function of the dream that it has to be experienced as reality. Moreover, it is understood as a wish-fulfilment, and this process of understanding occurs unconsciously. This was put in regard to a dream as follows (J. Sandler, 1976).

> We can elaborate on Freud's ideas of the wish striving for perceptual identify dream—by saying that the wish-fulfilment implicit in any surface expression of unconscious wishes or wishful fantasies is not only an outward expression, not only breakthrough irruption of the fulfilled unconscious wish in a disguised form, not only a centrifugal process. There is a centripetal wish in a disguised form, there is a centripetal element which is of equal importance. In order for the derivative to function as a wish-fulfilment, it has also to involve the perception of what has reached the surface. What I mean is simply this: The dream would be useless too the dreamer unless, at the time, he could also function as the observer of the dream. Similarly, a daydream would be valueless as a wish-fulfilment. That unless it was in some way perceived (perception should be distinguished from attention), A work of art would have no function in satisfying an unconscious wish unless the artist was aware of the act of creating and of the qualities of the creation itself. And even a symptom, regarded by Freud's for being formed as a derivative of the Unconscious in the form of a compromise-formation, would have no value as a wish fulfilment, if we followed this argument to its logical conclusion, unless the patient, at some level, perceived it.

What is important, is that the understanding work referred too applies not only to dreams, but to other forms of actualization, including certain symptoms (which can no longer be regarded simply as a breakthrough of expression on the surface of impulses arising from within the individual). Such symptoms cannot function as wish-fulfilment (using the term 'wish' in the broad sense indicated earlier) unless they are also perceived and unconsciously understood. There are many forms of actualization, delusional actualization, illusional actualization, symbolic actualizational delusional actualization, illusional actualization, symbolic

## Object Relations Theory

actualization, actualization by means of modifying one's own behaviour, actualization through modification of the external world, hallucinatory actualization, and so on. Actualization through conscious datadreams may also be satisfying, the degree to which the feeling of unreality of the datadream can be temporarily suspended. We have seen previously that the wish contains the representation of a role relationship, of a dialogue between extent that the wish contains a representation of a role relationship, of a dialogue between self and object playing a part. As a consequence, the extent that the wish contains an object relationship, every form of actualization will represent the fulfilment of a wished-for relationship. Thus, in our rel relationship, in our fantasies, in our artistic production, in our symptoms, in our dreams, in our play and perhaps, even, in our scientific productions, we may actualize unconscious wishful internal relationship in a symbolic form.

There is no doubt of the importance to us of a understanding of the ways in which individuals actualize the infantile object relationships present in their unconscious fantasies through many different activities in their daily lives. These activities may show themselves in relation to other people, or may simply be preset as so-called 'character traits.' Some character traits appear to be specifically designed to evoke particular responses in others, and this may give us an additional avenue of approach to the understanding of character.

In all this there is the implication that we can consider interpersonal relationships within the framework of our intrapsychic psychoanalytic psychology, by taking into account the various hidden ways in which people attempt to actualize their conscious and unconscious wishes and the object relationships inherent in the individual's wishful fantasies. Members of a group will 'negotiate' with one another in terms of the responses which each one needs and in terms of the responses which are demanded of him. The members of the group may even make unconscious 'deals' or 'transactions' in terms of the responses involved, so that each gains as much object-related wish-fulfilment as possible in return for concessions to other members of the group.

Summing up the views which have been put forward so far, we are found that the object relationship is seen as an intrapsychic relationship, depicted throughout are mental representations, and forming an intrinsic part of the wish or wishful fantasy. After a certain point in the child's development we cannot speak of a wish which does not have ideational content; and this ideational content is, for the purpose of our work, and often centred around the representation of oneself in interaction with the object. The object plays as an important a role as the self in the mental representation which is part of the wish. Not all wishes are instinctual wishes, but there are also wishes to gain or preserve safety and well-being to maintain control, and to defend against unpleasant feelings or the prospect of unpleasant feelings. In addition, we are constantly motivated too replenish a feeling of security, well-being or affirmation to gain a sort of nutriment or aliment to maintain a basic feeling of security and integrity. We do this almost automatically through the dialogue with the object in reality or in fantasy. If we see object relationship as wishfulfilments on a broad dense, then the fulfilment of an object (in reality, in fantasy, or both) which will act and react in the appropriate way. Just as the dream provides an identity of perception, as described by Freud (1900), so does the experience of the real or imagined object relationship provided an identity of perception, an identity of relation, in satisfying the wish. As in the dream,. And in other derivatives of unconscious wishes, the mental apparatuses may find very roundabout routes in order to obtain wish-fulfilment (And thus actualized a wished-for object relationship) through a disguised identity of perception.

To turn to the question of the development of object relationships, we can assume that a significant relationships begin to be built up in the mind of the child very early in life. We can assume that the infant is an experiencing animal, which it has a sensorium which is affected by stimuli from within (especially those arising form biological needs and instinctual drives) and also by stimuli from without, in particular those arising from the actions of the mother. Ths subjective experience which registers on the infant's sensorium, in the first instance predominantly feeling-states, although these are mixed with other sensations as well. The laying down of memory-traces and the organization of perceptual and memory structures gradually lead to further development of the infant's representational world, which acts as a basis for the ongoing organization of the child's subjective experience and motor activities. Naturally, the particular interaction which he has with external world, as well as his particular individual capacities, will exercise a profound influence on the development of the child's representational world. During the course of his early development he will create representation of his own self and his objects, and will later develop symbolic representation for use in thought and fantasy.

In the development of object relationships (i.e., of structure role relationships) the part played by affective experience in central. An experience only has or retains meaning for the child if it is linked with feeling. The assumption is made that ultimately all meaning is developmentally and functionally related to states of feeling, and that an experience which does not have some relation to a feeling-state has no psychological significance for the individual at all. This is in line with the view that we previously put forward on the role of feeling as psychic regulators (Sandler and Joffe, 1969).

We can speculate that, in the beginning, the child will have two great classes of subjective experience—those experiences which are pleasant, gratifying, comfortable, and associated with safety on the one hand and those which are unpleasant uncomfortable and painful on the other. The child naturally reacts to experiences which are either pleasurable or its opposite and apposing as to unpleasurable, as he perceives, in his own primitive way, as a pleasant one, associated with pleasant feelings, he will respond to it by joyful gurgling, and by other signs of happiness. If he is subjected to a situation which is painful or unpleasant he will show in a responds of withdrawal, distress both. If we, speak only in terms of recognition rather than of remembering, we could postulate that the first important distinction recognized by the child in the world of his experience is the difference between the two basic classes of affects, of feeling-experiences. Both are reacting to when the impinges upon the child, but in different and opposing ways. If we stretch the concept of 'object' a little further than usual, we could say that the first objects of the child are the experiencing of pleasure and satisfaction on the one hand, and those of unpleasure and pain on the other. In a sens, we could say that from very early, on the child begins to experience a dialogue with these primary objects, even though at first he may have no control over the dialogue.

That is to say: Pleasure is greeted by the child with joy and excitement, and the child will welcome it. Unpleasure, on the other hand, is greeted by primitive mechanisms of rejection, avoidance and withdrawal, by anger and even rage. These initial differentiated responses to the two major classes of experiences, the two primary 'objects' of the child, are, in the beginning, biologically based. They are not under the (conscious or unconscious) voluntary control of the infant, although his responses immediately affect the state of his sensorium and lead to the development and construction of further mental representations which come to be linked with the different feeling-states.

Thus, the first division of the child's world can be regarded as the division into pleasure and unpleasure as objects. Because the child is in constant interaction with his environment, and constantly receives a feedback from his environment, a response which is intimately associated with feelings of one sort or anther, he will attempt to maintain his relationship to the 'nice' or 'good' object as much as possible and minimize, to the extent that he can, his contact with the 'nasty' 'or 'bad' objects. All of this forces him into a dialogue with his subjective experiences, even though the boundaries between himself and others have not yet been created.

As other sensory and perceptual subjective experiences become associated with the primary affective objects, we, as we begin to get the formation of representations of objects in the sense of people or parts of people, and this includes the infant's own self representation. There seems to be an increasing amount of evidence that there is a given, inborn basis for the child's early responses to external objects, although there is no evidence that the child 'knows' the difference between 'internal' and 'external.' We can conceive of these early predispositions of the child as based on inborn organized perceptual and response tendencies related to potential object representations, just as there is evidence to postulate an inborn neurological substratum for the body scheme or body image (Weinstein, 1968). Recently as Newson and Newson (1975) have described how the children only achieve a fully articulated knowledge of his world as he becomes involved in social transactions with other communicating human beings. It has been shown (Bower, 1974) how the infant can manifest extremely complicated behavioural responses to external events and circumstances, and that eye-hand- and arm coordination exists early onto a greater degree that we would be expected, even from the first weeks of life. What is highly significant in all the studies of infant interaction with things and persons in their environment is the very young infant's dependence on experiencing appropriated sensorial and affective feedback. This applies not only to such ordinary things as reaching and grasping but in perfecting social interactions, even so, that the words of Newson and Newson, 1075 who say:

> Clearly, findings of this kind . . . suggest that infant at birth are already possessed of the necessary sensory, motor and neural equipment to make it possible for them to respond appropriately toward real objects in a three-dimensional world . . . At the sam e time, we need to treat with caution the suggestion . . . that the human infant is somehow inherently possessed in the 'knowledge' that seen objects are tangible. Behaviour, however complicated carries no necessary implication that th organism is capable of appreciating the ends toward which its own behaviour is directed.

They go on further, as saying,

> 'However accurately guided is the missile to able to seek out its target, we do not generally feel it necessary to credit the missile with having knowledge about the target.'

Recent work (e.g., Schaffer, 1971, 1974; Trevarthen, 1975; Condon and Sander, 1974) have shown that the human face of the infant's mother fascinates him almost from birth, and slowed-down video-recordings of an interacting mother-baby pair, shows that the different sensorimotor components of the infant's activity are highly synchronised with each other and that his action sequences are organized to that they can 'mesh,' with a high degree of precision, with similar patterns of action produced by the human caretaker. As Newson and Newson (1975) go further, as follows:

> The fact is that, from a very early age, that infants appear to be capable of taking part in dialogue-like exchanges with other human beings. Thus, when the adult talks to the infant, he displays all the complex gestural accompaniments that one normally expects of attentive listening: And when the adult pauses, the infant can reply with a fully articulated, gesturally animated, conversion-like response.

Recent work (e.g., Schaffer, 1971, 1974; Trevarthen, 1975; Condon and Sander, 1974) have shown that the human face of the infants mothers fascinates him almost from birth, and slowing-down video-recordings of an interacting mother-baby pair shows that the different sensorimotor components of the infants activities are highly synchronized with each other and that his action sequences are organized so that they can mesh,`with a high degree of precision, with similar patterns of action produced by the human caretaker. As Newson and Newson (1975) put it:

> The fact is that, from a very early age, infants appear to be capable of taking part in dialogue-like exchange with other human beings: Thus, when the adult talking to the infant, he displays all the complex gestural accompaniments that one normally expects of attentive listening, and when the adult pauses, the infant can reply with a fully articulated, gesturally animated, conversion-like responses.

Trevarthen and his colleagues have described the complex coordinated interaction between infant and caretaker as an innate intersubjectivity. Bentovim (1977) has given a valuable review of the relation of child development research findings to psychoanalytic theory.

After the formation of the child's 'primary affective object' his innate predisposition and his actual experience (including his awareness of his own responses, in a primitive way, after they have occurred and his social experience in the interaction with his mother) will lead him gradually to construct a further boundary. This is the boundary between his representation of his objects (primarily of the caretaking mother). In addition he will create increasingly complex representations of the interactions, the relationship, the dialogues between himself and his objects. The essential motivating forces prompting both ego development and the interrelated development of object relationships ultimately derive from the changes in the subject's affective experience, from changes in his relation to his primary affective objects. The economics involved are the economics of pleasant and unpleasant experiences. That is to say, in that, from earliest infancy the individual attempt to maintain his close, joyous and blissful relationship to the basic 'good' affective state, to a constellation of pleasure, well-being and feeling of safety. Simultaneously, he will attempt to obliterate from his experience the other major primary affective 'object,' i.e., unpleasure and pain. Incidently, this raises an interesting point, for we would take the view that the child does not initially try to get rid of feelings of unpleasure by projecting them into the 'external' world, but rather than the child simply tries to make them disappear.

In this context one could paraphrase Freud's remarks in his paper 'On Narcissism' (1914) about the development of ego from the state of 'primary narcissism' (which corresponds to closeness to or union with 'good feelings' as an object) as follows: The development of object relationships consists in a departure from the close primary relation to the affects of pleasure, well-being and security and gives rise to a vigorous attempt to recover that relationship. Part of this 'vigorous attempt' is the obliteration or removal of unpleasant or painful feelings, if at all possible. Wish to remove that which is unpleasant, to obliterated it, or to displace it so that it is disowned, mobilizes all the resources of the infant, including what we normally refer to as his aggression.

Inasmuch as there seems to be a predisposition from birth for the child to learn to experience the caretaking mother as a source of pleasure. He very quickly links his subjective experience of his interaction with her with the primary affective pleasurable object. We want to stress that it is not the mother that has yet become the 'good' or 'nice' object, but rather the dynamic gestalt of interaction experience arising from the interrelation between the child and his mother. With the later development of boundaries between self and object, the child will attempt to restore his relationship to the earlier pleasurable affective states, by making use of the dialogue which has developed between himself and his mother. He will make use of the 'mutual cueing' or 'perceptual refuelling' described so vividly by Mahler and her colleagues. This cueing or refuelling is a continuation of the dialogue which occurs from the earliest weeks of life. The refuelling dialogue (Sandler, 1977) leads to a relationship with the person as object which can be regarded as essentially a structured role-relationship, a complementary interaction between self and object:

> With the growth of self-object boundaries and the associated experience of separateness, the object gradually develops an identity of its own in the mind of the child, and it is the repeated scanning of that constant so-called 'libidinal' object, who interacts with the child, even at a distance, which provides a refuelling, a nutriment, an aliment from the child's senses of security and feeling of mastery . . . However, with self-object differentiation from the nondifferentiated state, another constant object, an object with an equally enduring identity, also emerges for the child. This is the child's own self . . . We are very aware of the infant's dialogue with his real object . . . But we have in flowing of a parallel process occurring . . . in which the child constantly and automatically scan and have a dialogue with his own self to get refuelling and affirmation, through the perception of cues, that his self is his own familiar self, that it is no stranger to him (A-M. Sandler, 1977).

In the absence of the object, the relationship can be re-created (after a certain point in development) as a dialogue in the child's conscious or unconscious fantasy life. As to emphasize, object relationships can be regarded as role relationships. This is as true of the relationships in thought or fantasy to the various images deriving from the structures as called 'introjection' or 'internalized objects' as of the relationships which obtain between the subject and persons perceived in his external environment.

We can broaden our theoretical base by placing emphasis on the child's wishful impulses and wishful fantasies (and not only on his instinctual drives) we would in continuation maintain:

(1) That needed and associated wishes are aroused by disturbances in the basic central (conscious or unconscious) feeling-state of the individual. Such disturbances are brought about not only by drive stimuli and internal conflict but also by the external world—for example, by the perception of the absence of the object who forms part of a crucial role-relationship, resulting in a lack of 'affirmation.'

(2) That wishes of all sorts contain the mental representation of self, of object, and of the interaction between the two. Again, the aim of such interactions is to bring about a way of closeness to the primary affective 'good' state or object, and distance form the primary affective 'bad' unpleasant state or object:

And,

(3) That the negotiations of early infancy continue into adult life, although we tend to become more and more inflexible in the roles we demand of others and of others.

While object relationships can be conceived of as wish-fulfilment, sometimes these are (of necessity) extremely heavily disguised wish-fulfilment. The overt relationship can be considered to be a derivative of an underlying wishful fantasy role-relationship. Often radically modified by defensive activities of one sort or another. Such defensive activity includes all the various forms of projection and externalization. But all these processes can be viewed as occurring intraphyically, as part of the internal work of defence and censorship. We can also include in such mental work processes, such as projective identification (Klein) and the use of the object as a 'container' (Bion), providing that we do not conceive of something actually and concretely being put into the other object, rather than some aspect of the subject's self representation is defensively placed (or displaced) intraphysically in fantasy or thought into the subject's mental representations of his object. The underlying object relationship, modified intraphysically by defensive processes, can then be actualized in a manifest form which may be very different from the unconscious fantasy relationship. The actualization can provide a wish-fulfilment because of the capacity for 'unconscious understanding work.' This allows an unconscious understanding of the real meaning of the manifest relationship to occur. While childhood relationships may be repeated without much alteration in later life, they may equally be heavily disguised, and it is part of the work of analysis to trace the ways in which this disguise has been created, i.e., to examine the defensive distortions of the original unconscious wishes and fantasies embodying the sought-for and gratifying role-relationship.

The clinical implications of the point of view presented, is such, that, in a primitive way to be far reaching. The regulation of conscious and unconscious feelings is placed in the centre of the clinical stage, as the interpretive clarification of the feeling-state which is closest to the surface, becoming a primary consideration in our technical approach, and we include, of what may be happening to the patient, the notion that his feeling-state may be affected by stimuli, from which are not necessarily instinctual by origin. And, we are provided with a view of motivation, conflict and possibly of psychopathology and symptoms, all of which determine the control of feelings through the direct or indirect maintenance of specific role relationships, which is of crucial significance.

# REFERENCES

- Bower, T. G. R. (1974). Development ion Infancy. San Francisco. Freeman.
- Bowlby, J. (1969) Attachment and Loss: Vol.1.Attachme t. London. Hogarth Press.
- Bowlby, J. (1973). Attachment and Loss; Vol 2. Separation, Anxiety and Anger. London Hogarth Press.
- Condon, W. S. & Sander. L. W. (1974). Neonate movement is synchronized with adult speech. Science (N.Y.) 183, 99-101.
- Freud, S. (1900). The interpretation of dreams. S.E. 4-5.
- Freud, S. (1914). On narcissism: an introduction. S.E. 14.
- Isaacs, S. (1948). The nature and function of phantasy. In: J. Psycho-Anal. 29, 73-97.
- Joffe, W. G. & Sandler, J. (1967). Some conceptual problems involved in the consideration of disorders of narcissism. J. Child Psychother. 2, 56-66.
- Klein M. (1932). The Psycho-Analysis of children. London; Hogarth Press
- Klein, M. (1957)., Envy and Gratitude. London: Tavistock Publ.
- Leweis, M. & Rosenblum, L. A. (1974). The effect of the Infant on its Caregiver. New York. Wiley.
- Mahler, M., Pine F. & Bergman, A. (1975) The Psychological Birth of the Human Infant. New York: Basic Books.
- Newson, J. & Newson, E. (1975). Intersubjectivity and the transmission. of culture: the social origins of symbolic functioning. Bull. Br. Psychol. Soc. 28, 437-446.
- Redford, E. N., Sander, L. W. & Shapiro, T. (eds.) (1976), Infant Psychiatry, New Haven: Yale Univ. Press.
- Sandler, A.-M. (1977). Beyond eight-month anxiety. Int. J. Psycho-Anal. 58, 195-207.
- Sandler, J. (1972). The role of affects in psychoanalytic theory. In Physiology, Emotion and Psychosomatic illness. (Ciba Found. Symp. 8, new series). Amsterdam: Elsevier-Excerpta Medica.
- Sandler, J. (1974). Physiological conflict and the structural model: some clinical and theoretical implications. Int. J. Psycho-Anal. 55, 53-62.
- Sandler, J. (1976a). Dreams, unconscious fantasies and identity of perception`. Int. Rev. Psycho-Anal. 3, 33-42.

* Sandler, J. (1976b). Countertransference and role-responsiveness. Int. Rev. PsychoAnal: 3, 43–47.
* Sandler, J.(1977). Actualization and object relationships. J. Philadelphia Ass. Psychoanal. 4, 59.
* Sandler, J. & Joffe, W. G. (1969). Towards as basic psychoanalytic model. Int. J. Psycho-Anal. 59, 79–90.
* Schaffer, H. R. (1971). The Growth of Sociability: Harmondsworth: Penguin.
* Schaffer, H. R. (1974). Behavioural synchrony in infancy. New Scientist 62, 16.
* Spitz, R. A. (1974). A Genetic Field Theory of Ego Formation. New York: Int. Univ. Press.
* Deutsch, H. Ueber Zufriedenheit, Glück und Ekstase. Internat. Ztschr. $f$. Psychosanal., 13: 410–419, 1927.
* Deutsch, H. Some forms of emotional disturbance and their relationship to schizophrenia. Psychoanal. Quart., 11: 301–321, 1942.
* Freud, A. The Ego and the Mechanisms of Defence. New York, Internat. Univ. Press. 1946.
* Freud, S. (1914) On narcissism: an introduction. Coll. Papers, 4: 30–59. London Hogarth Press, 1925.
* Freud, S. (1917) Mourning and melancholia. Ibid., 4: 152–170.
* Freud, S. (1922) Group Psychology and the analysts of the Ego. London: Hogarth Press, 1940.
* Freud, S. (1931). Female sexuality. Coll. Papers, 5: 252–272. London. Hogarth Press. 1950.
* Hartmann, H. Comments in the psychoanalytic theory of the ego. The Psychoanalytic Study of the child, 5:4–96. New York. Interna. Univ. Press, 1950.
* Lampi-de Groot. J. Problems of femininity; Psychoanal, Qua t, 2: 489–518, 1933.
* Lewin, B. D, The body.

# CHAPTER FIVE

# Narcissistic Object Choice in Women

Narcissus of the Greek mythology, holds in that of a youth, the son of the river god Cephissus. Because of his great beauty many women fell in love with Narcissus, but he repulsed their advances. Among the lovelorn maidens was the nymph Echo, who had incurred the displeasure of Hera and had been condemned by the goddess never to speak again except to repeat what was said to her. Echo was therefore unable to tell Narcissus of her love, but one day, as Narcissus was walking in the woods, he became separated from his companions. When he shouted, 'Is anyone here?' Echo joyfully answered, 'Here, here.' Unable to see her hidden among the trees, Narcissus cried 'Come!' Back came the answer, 'Come, come,' as Echo stepped forth from the woods with outstretched arms. Narcissus cruelly refused to accept Echo's love; she was so humiliated that she hid in a cave and wasted away until nothing was left of her but her voice. To punish Narcissus, the avenging goddess Nemesis made Narcissus fall hopelessly in love with his own beautiful face as he saw it reflected in a pool. As he gazed in fascination, unable to remove himself from his image, he gradually pined away. At the place where his body had lain grew a beautiful flower, honouring the name and memory of Narcissus.

People with narcissistic personality disorder have a grandiose sense of self-importance. They seek excessive admiration from others and fantasize about unlimited success or power. They believe they are special, unique, or superior to others. However, they often have very fragile self-esteem.

People with depression often experience feelings of worthlessness, helplessness, guilt, and self-blame. They may interpret a minor failing on their part as a sign of incompetence or interpret minor criticism as condemnation. Some depressed people complain of being spiritually or morally dead. The mirror seems to reflect someone ugly and repulsive. Even a competent and decent person may feel deficient, cruel, stupid, phony, or guilty of having deceived others. People with major depression may experience such extreme emotional pain that they consider or attempt suicide. At least 15 percent of seriously depressed people commit suicide, and many more attempt it.

Personality disorders are mental illnesses in which one's personality results in personal distress or a significant impairment in social or work functioning. In general, people with personality disorders have poor perceptions of themselves or others. They may have low self-esteem or overwhelming narcissism, poor impulse control, troubled social relationships, and inappropriate emotional responses. Considerable controversy exists over where to draw the distinction between a normal personality and a personality disorder.

Freud's paper 'On Narcissism: An Introduction' has a special place within the frame of his work: It is the forerunner of ego psychology. A number of problems which later are dealt with from the point of view of ego psychology are treated on the basis of libido theory.

Narcissism means the cathexis of the own self with libido, as the term 'self' is used because the state of primary narcissism exists only prior to any ego differentiation, a point made by Hartmann. In what is called secondary narcissism as later return of object cathexis to the own person.

Freud's paper says that the instinctual aim in narcissism is to be loved. Most pregenital aims are of this nature. Objects, at that level, are 'selfishly' used for one's own 'gratification,' their interests cannot yet be considered. Pregenital behaviour, incidentally, shows similar trait s in both sexes. Whether we define such behaviour as fixated on pregenital loves of object relationship, yet narcissistic, are a question of terminology.

The separation between self and object world develops gradually. In early phases of object relationship, objects exist only temporarily and are dropped after gratification has occurred, or destroyed in violent rage when they withhold gratification. Objects are experienced as part of the own body, inside and outside are constantly fused. Thus, we should use the term 'narcissistic' in concentrating on certain conditions:

(1) When body cathexis predominates and the own body is treated like a love object.
(2) When a fixation has occurred on a level on which the differentiation between ego and object is very diffuse, and primary identifications prevail instead of object love, and:
(3) When infantile ideas of, or longing for, omnipotence was either not outgrown or regressively revived, and problems of regulation of self-esteem a about there predominant. Such conditions are characteristic by a state of narcissistic want and are mostly caused by narcissistic injury.

When Freud states in his paper 'On Narcissism' that women are generally more narcissistic than men, it seems as though he were largely thinking of a fixation at some early levels of object relationship. At these early love levels, passive attitudes are more frequently found than an active reaching out for an object. He states that in contrast of the love object, the predominant sexual aim of women is to be loved. This, Freud stresses, applies particularly to the 'truest type' of women, who is primarily preoccupied with her physical beauty. By very reason of her narcissism this type of woman is attractive to men, because narcissistic self-admiration is enchanting to those who themselves had to give up this gratification long ago in the course of their development. The narcissistic interest in the own self should, by the way, be distinguished from the physiologically passive sexual aims of female sexuality which are frequently connected with love of the anaclitic type.

Our increased knowledge about the preoedipal development of children has taught us that this passive-narcissistic attitudes—even in those of women who really belong to the type defined by Freud—by no means represent a primary fixation on the infantile level. Freud and others (Mack Brunswick, II; Lamp-de Griot, 9) has described ho w, after the original oral and anal passivity, the young woman goes through a period of active pregenital—well as phallic—attitudes in relation to the mother. This active person is brought to an abrupt end by the trauma of the discovery of the difference of the sexes. One of the possible solutions of the ensuing conflict is regression into the aforementioned pregenital, 'narcissistic' passivity or demandingness. In many cases, on the other hand, the phallic level is never relinquished and the fantasy of possessing a penis persists. Numerous women continue to have masculine longings which find expression in many ways, frequently in the form of inferiority feelings and a specific, unrealizable ambitions and ideals. A solution to such conflicts is sometimes reached through a specific choice of a love object representing what these young women originally wanted to be, and which they can love on this basis. An object that is different from the self, but which has qualities' they once desired for themselves, representing a narcissistic object choice. About this type, Freud wrote: 'The sexual ideal' (i.e., the idealized sex object) 'may enter into an interesting auxiliary relationship to the ego ideal. Where narcissistic gratification encounters actual hindrance, the sexual ideal may be used as a substitute gratification. In such a case a person loves (in conformity with the narcissistic type of object-choice) someone whom he once was, and no longer is, or else someone who possesses excellence which he never had at all . . . whoever possesses an excellence which the ego lacks for the attainment of its ideal, becomes loved.'

Narcissistic object choice of this kind is intended to undo a narcissistic trauma of castration, and to undo a state of narcissistic wants. The fact that such an object choice is a narcissistic one does not ye t make it pathologic. There are flowing transitions. As everywhere, from the normal to the pathologic.

Normal cases of this kind are well known. There are many women who replaced their original wish for a penis by developing male character traits and interest. If these character traits later on prove incompatible with their femininity, it becomes a good solution if they can love the same traits in a male object. In this way they can form a durable and stable relationship with men whose achievements, standards, and so on, they identify. These women thus love men who represent their own externalized, former ego identifications.

Other women, particularly those who were unable to sublimate their masculine wishes, retain constant, unrealizable masculine ambitions. Their identifications did not effect any change in the ego, but remain restricted to the ego ideal. It is obvious that any conspicuous pathology of the identifications and particularly any pathology of these special layers of identifications, of the ego ideal, will contribute to the pathology of the narcissistic object choice and object relationship.

Frequently, the object represents a composite of both these forms of identifications. Object choices based upon the externalizations of the second type lead more often to pathology than do object choices based upon the first.

Among the many interesting clinical entities representing pathological forms of narcissistic object choice, owe in considering of two basic groups of women who are in particular relations of dependent subservience to one man. The second group consists of women who have short-live, dependent infatuations during which the completely take over the man's personality, only to drop him again after a short time and to 'deify' another object. The rapid changes of personality and love objects and, all emotions of these young women have a spurious character. Wherefore, these two types impress one as complete opposites, however, there are certain similarities. In both of them the pathology is caused by the underlying pathological identifications which have been externalized.

## EXTREME SUBMISSIVENESS IN WOMEN

Often these women are deeply attached to one man, who to them is outstanding and great. Usually, some masculine characteristic is stressed: Either the man's physical strength, attractiveness, sex appeal, or his power, importance of intelligence, creativity, and so on. The woman feels that she cannot live without this partner, in order to maintain the relationship, she is willing to bear anything and, masochistically, to make all kinds of sacrifices.

Such women suffer from intense inferiority feelings. They are over-critical of themselves, and the admired qualities of the partner represent what they felt unable to attain for themselves in childhood and adolescence when only masculine values were of importance to them. The predominance of male identification is evidenced by the frequent, in such cases, of early daydreams with an all-male cast, i.e., the daydreamer herself appears as a boy, often without being conscious of her own identification with the hero. Girls are considered too uninteresting and ugly to be used at all for fantasy purposes. One such patient's daydream, for instance, dealt exclusively with a sadomasochistic relationship of a son with a grandiose father, the patient alternately identifying with both these fantasy objects.

Later on the sexual partner becomes the representative of the grandiose component of these masculine ambitions. It is very striking that in many of these cases the partner's body as a whole has to have phallic features. 'He has to be tall, lean and silken.' 'His body has to look like that of a Greek athlete.' Or: 'He has to be strong, upright, and broad-shouldered.' These traits are equally predominant in the daydream heros of adolescence. The patient whose sadomasochistic daydream becomes aware in the analysis that during intercourse she felt as though she were the man with the phallus-like body making love to her, the girl.

The narcissistic gain of such an identification is obvious. It results in feeling of oneness, of being one body with the grandiose sex partner, a feeling which is the complete opposite, as are the component ambitions based upon the grandiosity under the influence. However, over-strong feelings of ugliness and inferiority that predominated when his girl evaluated her personality by herself. It is obvious that a separation from such a partner is intolerable; it leads to a feeling of complete castration and has to be prevented by all means.

In several cases of this type, a sortal method of magic as restoring self-esteem could be particularly observed in the feeling of ecstasy accompanying orgasm. In this state it was as though the woman's individuality had ceases to exist; she felt herself flow together with the man. This, nonetheless, can be compared to what Freud calls the 'oceanic feeling'—the flowing together of self and world, of self and primary object. It has to do with a temporary relinquishment of the separating boundaries between ego, id and ego ideal. A unity with the ego ideal, which equals the unrealizable longing to be like an admired early object, is thus reached for these passing moments. It was obvious that the sex partner represented the personification of such a very phallic ego ideal. Grandiose masculinity was gained through the ecstatic intercourse.

In the analysis, the phallic object with whom this mystic identification occurred could be traced back to the father. We are dealing with an ego ideal of the paternal type. In these instances, the phallic features of the ideal were conspicuous; they completely overshadow any individual trait of the father as a person. One might say that this type of ego ideal is characterized by regressive, primitive traits as, (1) By its grandiosity (2) identification with an organ, and (3) the tendency to undo inferiority feelings through flowing together with a stronger object: That is to say, that through regression to any primitive form of object relationship, going back to a time in which ego boundaries were not yet stable and whatever appeared to be pleasurable and strong in the outside world could easily be experienced as belonging to the self.

As is not surprising in persons with such regressive traits, in a number of cases analysis showed that the fantasy of becoming one with a grandiose love partner was related to the original homosexual object, the mother, the primitive attachments to whom had never been relinquished. The undisguised phallic character of the later fantasy represented a subsequent addition, as a reaction to the disappointment at the lack of a penis in the mother.

The masochistic subservience is the outcome of the woman's need to hold on to the object at any cost.

This situation, however, is complicated by a number of factors. It is obvious that girls with a particular, narcissistic structure—i.e., with particular, grandiose ego ideals—are necessarily in a difficult position. No object really can live up to the grandiosity of the narcissistic demand. They must, as to say, to inflate the partner in order that he might meet their standard. Whatever contradicts the fantasy now has to be denied, and a great deal of countercathexis becomes necessary to hold on to the inflated image of the love object. This state of affairs is further complicated by the necessity to keep in check aggressive tendencies against the man who is, after all, in possession of the masculinity that the woman originally desired. Even greater overinflation of the love object is needed to counterbalance this aggression. This underlying ambivalence causes such women furtively to which and evaluates the partner. There is a constant doubt whether the man is really as wonderful as he is supposed to be, the warded-off aggression frequently is transformed into the aforementioned masochistic behaviour.

Relationships of this kind impress the superficial observer as specially 'real' forms of love. Only analysis reveals their infantile, narcissistic character. Not infrequently, women who need this type of relationship are otherwise well-integrated personalities. They maintain a critical self-evaluation and accurate reality testing. Infantile megalomanic longings shine through only in their attitude toward love objects, but do not otherwise appear in their personality structure. Greatness, so to speak, is completely ceded to the partner; union with him is their only way of establishing a feeling of this kind.

At this point a few remarks should be added about the ego ideal and its relation to the regulation of self-esteem. The formation of the ego ideal has from its very beginning to do with the keeping up of self-esteem. As his sense of reality grows, the child, recognizing his own weakness, endows his parents with the omnipotence he has had to forego. From this time on, desires set in to become like a glorified parent. The deep longing to become like the parent creates a constant inner demand upon the child's ego: An ego is formed. In cases of insufficient acceptance of reality the differentiation between ego and ego ideal may remain diffuse, and under certain conditions magic identifications with their glorified parent—megalomanic feelings—may replace the wish to be like him.

Such ego ideals should be distinguished from the concept of the superego. The superego represents a taking over of the parental do's and don't's. In spite of childish misunderstandings, the formation of the superego is based upon acceptance of reality. The ego ideal, on the other hand, is based upon the desire to cling in some form or another to a denial of the ego's, as well as of the parent's limitations and to regain infantile omnipotence by identifying with the idealized parent.

Nunberg differentiated in a similar way between ego ideal and superego. He believes that the ego ideal is formed earlier and is based upon identifications with the mother, prompted by love for her, where the later fear of the father leads to formation of the superego. Nunberg also stresses the greatest closeness of the superego to instead mastery and reality adjustment: While leaving to that which feelings are respectively role played by father or mother in the formation of the ego instances is dependent on their particular characteristics. One can describe the ego ideal as the earlier structure, as the precursor of the superego. Such examples as:

(1) In such cases ideas about the parental magnificence sometimes are completely fused with desires for a particular organ of the object, upon which the entire cathexis is concentrated. This is originally the breast or, somewhat later, the parental phallus. In the phallic phase a great deal of libidinal-narcissistic cathexis is concentrated on the penis and may spread over the whole body. It is at this period that the fantasy of the whole body being a phallus origination. Such that Lewin has described that fantasy as being alway based on oral incorporation. Body narcissism of particular intensity appears invariably combined with this fantasy. Its purpose of combatting castration anxiety is obvious. This condition probably represents the basis of the fact that the ego ideal of particularly narcissistic persons with deep fixations and insufficient faculty of desexualization is to be the paternal phallus. This may be compared to a stage in which the ego did not perceive the object as a whole, and identification was limited to the imitation of gesture. Instead of identification with the quality of the object, there predominate with the wish to be identified with an organ of the object. It is obvious how far such an ego ideal is removed from any possibility of realization.
(2) Not infrequently the ego ideal tinged with features of grandiosity, since it is based upon wishes to identify with a parent who is seen in a very infantile way.

In normal development these ideals gradually are modified. With the growing acceptance of reality the image of the parent becomes more and more realistic, superego elements gain importance and become fused with the ideal, and—most important—ego capacities are developed for the translation of inner demands into organized activities. A persistence of intensely narcissistic ego ideals obviously represents serious pathology. The formation of such ideals is a regular process of development; normally, however, they do not endure in their infantile form. Persistence of a megalomanic ego ideal is not caused by one isolated traumatic incident but by an overall weakness of the ego, immaturity of the superego, and early disturbances of object relationship. This latter factor is usually the most conspicuous. It is as though early disturbances had prevented the libido from attaching itself to objects, so that too much cathexis remains with the ego ideal. An over-grandiose ego ideal—combined, as not infrequently is, with inadequate talent s and insufficient ego strength—leads to intolerable inner conflicts and feelings of insufficiency. The reattachment of this ideal to an outside object and the reunion with the initiation by which of their sexual union, as in the case of subservient women, thus represents an undoing of a feeling of narcissistic wants, which coincides with the undoing of castration.

## TRANSITORY PSEUDO-INFATUATIONS: "AS IF" TYPES

In contrast to the submissive-dependent woman who often clings to one object throughout life, the other type shows a similar overvaluation of the object, with signs of deep dependency, merely for a limited time; these women 'fall in love' with men whom they 'deify' and without whom they consider life unbearable. They take over the man's personality, interests and values completely; it is as if they had no judgement of their own, no ego of their own. Bu t suddenly, after a short time, and thus elevated object are dethroned again. He is regarded as valueless, inferior, and dropped like a hot potato; and at the same time, the identification with hin is relinquished. Often this dropping of one object coincides with turning to a new one who is now elevated instead, only to be exchanged, in turn, for yet another after some time. However, the devaluation of any object is accompanied by a feeling of degradation of the own personality, which can be overcome only through the idealization and acquisition of a new object.

In such cases it seems as though the intensity of the feelings were spurious and unreal. In her very interesting paper, dealing with the 'as if' personality, Helene Deutsch describes a number of cases characterised by precisely this type of behaviour. In her cases as well in those of others have observed, the 'as if' pattern emerged in the relationship to objects as well as to causes of thoughts. The patients spuriously fell in and out of love in the course of a few days. Similarly, whenever they were under someone 's influence, they would for a short time is enthusiastically religious, or fanatically communistic, and whatever. The 'as if' behaviour relationship during childhood, due to unfavourable family situations. They were incapable of loving anybody and only could relate to external objects, such that relations came through primitive forms of identification. Of course, such relationships have no continuity. Each identification is followed by another, and all relationships and emotions are spurious and impermanent. Helene Deutsch points out that the rapid sequence of identifications may be understood as a method to appease extreme objects by becoming like them. She also stresses the deficient faculty of sublimation, ego weakness, and lacking internalization of the superego. Furthermore, it appears that the rapidly changing identification has the function of undoing narcissistic injuries. In a magic way narcissistic compensation is gained and, simultaneously, a substitute for the lacking object relationships.

Again, as in the cases of subservient women, we find to the exaggerated, grandiose ego ideal which is unrealizable. Precisely because there is always an early disturbance of object relationship and the libido could not be placed in a normal way, the narcissistic structure, the ego ideal, is over cathected, but there is an essential difference between the two types. Submissive women of the first group need men with definite qualities that have a high value for these girl, since early childhood and present well-internalized identification. By contrast, the women of the 'as if' type show a lack of discrimination in the choice of objects. Some of them can glorify anything and are ready to identify themselves with anyone happening to enter their sphere of life. In the case of others, their admiration is tied to one condition: The man's worth must be recognized by other people. The content of his qualities irrelevant, these identifications are not really internalized; they are superficial imitations. Relevant to only the endeavour to achieve greatness in this way.

It has been stressed repeatedly that the identifications seen in this type of patient are highly pathologic. It has been said that they consist of superficial imitations instead of deeply internalized transformations of the personality. Identifications of this type are characteristic for an early stage of development.

Identifications are older than object love. They form the first bridge from the self to the world. Through identification, the strange and therefore disturbing outside objects are assimilated ('digested') and thereby made pleasurable. One of the mechanics of this primary taking-into-the-self consists in imitating the outside object. The oral incorporation takes place at the same time, or shortly before. Imitation is an ego activity, oral incorporations libidinal processes. The interrelation between the two procedure was non e too clear, nonetheless, this magic method—the imitative gesture, as Berta Bornstein calls it—can be considered a prestige of identification. This primitive identification can take place with many objects and not only with 'loved' ones. Whatever is impressive at the moment is imitated. This implies that such initial identifications are transitory at first. It is only by manifold and long exposure that any lasting identification comes about. Stable relationships to beloved objects greatly facilitated such development. New skills, interests and patterns of behaviour are developed. For a time the child was the father when he put on his father's coat and played at driving the car. Normally, this stage is gradually outgrown. The child not only makes noises but learns to talk; he not only holds a newspaper, like his father but learns to read. Thus he leans to master reality and acquires a capacity for sound reality testing. These now stable identifications are, so to speak, the building materials from which the ego is made.

In the course of development, a differentiation takes place between identification and love. Objects different from the self can be loved without the need to take over their qualities, and, on the other hand, identification with objects as whole person, real ego transformation, is achieved. A great many of these identifications are based on the desexualization—or, as Hartmann puts it, the neutralization—of libido, thus leading to real sublimations which are not reversible even under unfavourable conditions. On the other hand, a fixation at a level of immature ego identification, of transitory imitations, of playing at being something instead of rally becoming it, amounts to serious pathology. A regression of this state can, for instance, be seen in schizophrenics to whom imitation of gestures stands for being something.

However, such a woman's dependence on the man has to be understood as an immature relationship of a weak ego to an object that is seen as strong and as powerful as the parent was seen by the infant. It is a symptom of insufficient superego development.

This immaturity of the superego may find expression not in dependency on the judgment of one object, closer investigation frequently reveals a dependence onto the judgment of various homosexual objects, i.e., in many cases the dependence on the material judgment has never been displaced to men. Even so, this situation as well as dependency on men must be distinguished from the projection of a well-circumscribed and often overly-strict superego onto the love objects. Projection of the superego does not seem to be more characteristic of either sex. Some persons with intense—inner conflicts try to solve their internal tensions by reprojecting the critical superego onto external objects whose benevolence and forgiveness are now sought for. Sometimes in such cases one finds that a real, psychotic loss of object relationship had taken place at some point, and that the projection of the superego is an attempt at restitution. This mechanism must be strictly distinguished from those which we wish to investigate.

Just like the superficiality of the identifications on the imitation level, the dependence on outside judgment facilitates the abandoning of objects. This does not yet explain, nonetheless, why with the relinquishment of such a relationship the former object so often suddenly evokes s disgust or hatred, instead of admiration, nor why with process is connected with such a sudden drop in self-esteem.

Sudden changes of mood and of self-esteem, from the feeling of grandiosity to that of nothingness are characteristic of an infantile ego. Such vacillations of mood appear regularly in early phases. They represent the shift from gratifications=omnipotence to hunger=extreme feeling of powerlessness. At that stage, no degree of self-assurance exists, shading of good and bad, great and small, require a greater acceptance of reality, an ability too stand tension to wait for gratification, to judge and think without being overwhelmed by desires and emotion. Just as tolerance toward others is a late and complicated achievement, tolerance and objective appraisal in relation to the own self, likewise a late acquisition of maturity.

Normally, these extreme vacillations are stabilized through some gratification coming from the objects. We know, moreover, that by identification with the powerful parent the child restores his narcissistic balance in a magic way. These narcissistic desires to take the place of the parent coincide, normally, with a positive attachment to the object. But, if there is no consistency of relationship to the object, or if objects are really lacking, or if aggressive feeling or a particular ambivalence prevails. Then his negative, devaluing attitude will destroy the object as well as the ego ideal which is formed in his pattern. The tiniest of frustrations, or any devaluation of the object by a third party, will not only undermine the child's own self-esteem, i.e., his feeling of power. But unleash relentless hostility against the object and against any ideal of the object, which the child is trying to establish in himself. Then the vacillation of mood does not stop before the object that represents the externalized, narcissistic ideal. The ego-ideal-object is loved, elevated imitated for a short while, but after the slightest disappointment it is immediately hated, destroyed, abandoned. Whereas, when an object is loved and admired, its splendour falls through narcissistic identification upon the ego, as aggression against the object—the 'shadow of the object', as Freud formulated it in 'Mourning and Melancholia'—falls upon the ego.

However, in contrast to what happens in melancholic depression, the identification of the imitation level can be stopped at will. The shadow can be cast off at once, most easily by turning to a new object and starting a new relationship; the mood of dejection, too, is only transitory.

The described phenomenon does not constitute all the existing varieties of narcissistic object choice in women, nonetheless, they may be considered particularly important. The various forms of narcissistic disturbances need further investigation.

Such has of occurring, is the supporting reinforcing stimulus for which of a brief summation has, in, at least, an inclined inclination for arriving as a logical consequence:

(1) The ego ideal, in contrast to the superego, is based upon a narcissistic identification with the parent, which is seen in an infantile, glorified way. Persistence of particular, grandiose ideals has to do with disturbances of object relationship and ego development.
(2) Unsublimated sexual features of the ideal, expressed in the fantasy of becoming the paternal (or, sometimes, maternal) phallus, represent a special, regressive trait.
(3) Fixation on the level of imitative gesture lead s to a lack of internalization in the ego ideal and constitute the basis for the 'as if' personality,
(4) The impact of narcissistic inquiries, such as, in women, the becoming aware of the difference of the sexes, may lead to a regressive revival of primitive, narcissistic ego ideals.
(5) The externalization of such an ego ideal, and its fusion with a lover object, represents a form of narcissistic object choice in women.
(6) The degree of pathology of the narcissistic object choice depends on the normalcy or pathology of the ego ideal.
(7) Need for identification, not infrequently in the form of ecstatic-orgastic flowing together with the idealized object, can become the basis for a subservient relationship of a woman to a man?
(8) The masochistic element in such subservience is frequently based on the overcompensation of aggressive feeling against the man.
(9) Idealization and identification with the idealized object may represent the only available form of substitution for the lacking ability to form object relationships.
(10) A greater degree of disturbance of the ego ideal frequently goes hand in hand with an insufficiently developed superego and leads to dependence upon 'public opinion' or a specific third persons.

(11) Sudden, aggressive demolition of idealized figures, combine with depressive lowering of self-esteem, is based upon a predominance of aggression against the objects on whom the ego ideal is built.

# REFERENCES

- Deutsch. H. Ueber Zufriedenheit, Glück und Ekstase. Internat. Ztschr. *f*. Psychoanal., 13: 410-419, 1927.
- Deutsch, H. Some forms of emotional disturbance and their relationship to schizophrenia. Psychoanal. Quar t., 11: 301-321.1942.
- Freud, A. The Ego and the Mechanism of Defence. New York: Internal. Univ. Press, 1946.
- Freud, S. (1914) On narcissism: an introduction. Coll. Papers, 4: 30-59. London Hogarth Press, 1925.
- Freud, S. (1917) Mourning and melancholia. Introduction., 4: 152-170.
- Freud, S. !1922) Group Psychology and the Analysis of the Ego. London: Hogarth Press. 1940.
- Freud, S. (1931) Female sexuality. Coll. Papers,. 5: 252-272. London: Hogarth Press. 1950.
- Hartmann, H. Comments On the Psychoanalytic theory of the ego. The psychoanalytic Study of the ego. The Psychoanalytic Study of the Child, 5: 74-96. New York: Internat. Univ. Press, 1950.
- Lampi-de Groot, J. Problems of femininity, Psychoanal. Quart., 2: 489-518, 1953.
- Lewis, B. D. The body as phallus. Ibid., 2: 24-47, 1933.
- Mack Brunswick, R. The premedical phase of libido development. Idid., 9: 293-319. 1940.
- Nunberg, H. Allegemeine Neurosenlehre, Bern: Huber, 1932.
- Reich, A. Contributions to the psychoanalysis of extreme submissiveness in women. Psychoanasl. Quart., 9: 470-480. 1940.

# CHAPTER SIX

# Structural Derivatives of Object Relationships

Reasons that have posited the observation of some peculiar defensive operations that are set in patients suffering from severe character disorder and so called 'borderline' conditions (Knight, 1954). There is a kind of 'selective' impulsivity shown by many borderline patients, especially those suffering from 'acing out' character disorder with some borderline features. Ingesting the observation that the apparent lack of impulse control of these patients is often of a particular, selective kind. Some patients may present very good impulse control in all but one area. In this one area, there may exist rather than lack of impulse control, alternative activation of contradictory manifestations of the patient of such an impressive nature that one comes to feel that there is a compartmentalization of the entire psychic life of the patient. For example, a patient shown constant switching between severe fears in regard to sexual activity at times and an impulse ridden sexual behaviour, at other times, both alternating conditions being temporarily ego syntonic during their respective appearance. Another patient appeared to be lying 'impulsively' at times, at other times he gave the impression of feeling guilty or ashamed of lying, and insisted that lying was no longer a problem for him and angrily accused other people (the therapist) of lying. What was striking was the complete separation of the time that the 'impulse' lying occurred, from the times the patient remembered the lying but would feel no longer emotionally connected with it and, on the contrary, was strongly convinced that lying was no longer part of his psychic reality. This patient presents that both the lying and the 'anti-lying' episodes were psychic manifestations of one global, rigid characterlogical pattern.

Incidently, people with borderline personality disorder experience intense emotional instability, particularly in relationships with others. They may make frantic efforts to avoid real or imagined abandonment by others. They may experience minor problems as major crises. They may also express their anger, frustration, and dismay through suicidal gestures, self-mutilation, and other self-destructive acts. They tend to have an unstable self-image or sense of self.

As children, most people with this disorder were emotionally unstable, impulsive, and often bitter or angry, although their chaotic impulsiveness and intense emotions may have made them popular at school. At first they may impress people as stimulating and exciting, but their relationships tend to be unstable and explosive.

About 2 percent of all people have borderline personality disorder. About 75 percent of people with this disorder are female. Borderline personalities are at high risk for developing depression, alcoholism, drug dependence, bulimia, dissociative disorders, and post-traumatic stress disorder. As many as 10 percent of people with this disorder commit suicide by the age of 30. People with borderline personality disorder are among the most difficult to treat with psychotherapy, in part because their relationship with their therapist may become as intense and unstable as their other personal relationships.

The personality disorder conditions and associated anxiety their must in attendance to evaluate the guiding principles to the current concepts of 'personality disorder' that have taken on the colouration of an atypically depiction such the 'Personality Disorders,' are disorders in which one's personality results in personal distress or significantly impair social or work functioning. Every person has a personality—that is, a characteristic way of thinking, feeling, behaving, and relating to others. Most people experience at least some difficulties and problems that result from their personality.

The specific point at which those problems justify the diagnosis of a personality disorder is controversial. To some extent the definition of a personality disorder is arbitrary, reflecting subjective as well as professional judgments about the person's degree of dysfunction, needs for change, and motivation for change.

Personality disorders involve behaviour that deviates from the norms or expectations of one's culture. However, people who pervert from cultural norms are not necessarily dysfunctional, nor are people who conform to cultural norms necessarily healthy. Many personality disorders represent extreme variants of behaviour patterns that people usually value and encourage. For example, most people value confidence but not arrogance, agreeableness but not submissiveness, and conscientiousness but not perfectionism.

Because no clear line exists between healthy and unhealthy functioning, critics question the reliability of personality disorder diagnoses. A behaviour that seems deviant to one person may seem normal to another depending on one's gender, ethnicity, and cultural background. The personal and cultural biases of mental health professionals may influence their diagnoses of personality disorders.

An estimated 20 percent of people in the general population have one or more personality disorders. Some people with personality disorders have other mental illnesses as well. About 50 percent of people who are treated for any psychiatric disorder have a personality disorder.

Mental health professionals rarely diagnose personality disorders in children because their manner of thinking, feeling, and relating to others does not usually stabilize until young adulthood. Thereafter, personality traits usually remain stable. Personality disorders often decrease in severity as a person ages.

Two of the most common personality disorders, antisocial personality disorder and borderline personality disorder. It also provides brief descriptions of other types of personality disorders.

People with antisocial personality disorder act in a way that disregards the feelings and rights of other people. Antisocial personalities often break the law, and they may use or exploit other people for their own gain. They may lie repeatedly, act impulsively, and get into physical fights. They may mistreat their spouses, neglect or abuse their children, and exploit their employees. They may even kill other people. People with this disorder are also sometimes called sociopaths or psychopaths. Antisocial behaviour in people less than 18 years old is called conduct disorder.

Antisocial personalities usually fail to understand that their behaviour is dysfunctional because their ability to feel guilty, remorseful, and anxious is impaired. Guilt, remorse, shame, and anxiety are unpleasant feelings, but they are also necessary for social functioning and even physical survival. For example, people who lack the ability to feel anxious will often fail to anticipate actual dangers and risks. They may take chances that other people would not take.

Antisocial personality disorder affects about 3 percent of males and 1 percent of females. This is the most heavily researched personality disorder, in part because it costs society the most. People with this disorder are at high risk for premature and violent death, injury, imprisonment, loss of employment, bankruptcy, alcoholism, drug dependence, and failed personal relationships.

People with borderline personality disorder experience intense emotional instability, particularly in relationships with others. They may make frantic efforts to avoid real or imagined abandonment by others. They may experience minor problems as major crises. They may also express their anger, frustration, and dismay through suicidal gestures, self-mutilation, and other self-destructive acts. They tend to have an unstable self-image or sense of self.

About 2 percent of all people have borderline personality disorder. About 75 percent of people with this disorder are female. Borderline personalities are at high risk for developing depression, alcoholism, drug dependence, bulimia, dissociative disorders, and post-traumatic stress disorder. As many as 10 percent of people with this disorder commit suicide by the age of 30. People with borderline personality disorder are among the most difficult to treat with psychotherapy, in part because their relationship with their therapist may become as intense and unstable as their other personal relationships.

Avoidant personality disorder is social withdrawal due to intense, anxious shyness. People with avoidant personalities are reluctant to interact with others unless they feel certain of being liked. They fear being criticized and rejected. Often they view themselves as socially inept and inferior to others.

Dependent personality disorder involves severe and disabling emotional dependency on others. People with this disorder have difficulty making decisions without a great deal of advice and reassurance from others. They urgently seek out another relationship when a close relationship ends. They feel uncomfortable by themselves.

People with histrionic personality disorder constantly strive to be the centre of attention. They may act overly flirtatious or dress in ways that draw attention. They may also talk in a dramatic or theatrical style and display exaggerated emotional reactions.

People with narcissistic personality disorder have a grandiose sense of self-importance. They seek excessive admiration from others and fantasize about unlimited success or power. They believe they are special, unique, or superior to others. However, they often have very fragile self-esteem.

Obsessive-compulsive personality disorder is characterized by a preoccupation with details, orderliness, perfection, and control. People with this disorder often devote excessive amounts of time to work and productivity and fail to take time for leisure activities and friendships. They tend to be rigid, formal, stubborn, and serious. This disorder differs from obsessive-compulsive disorder, which often includes more bizarre behaviour and rituals.

People with paranoid personality disorder feel constant suspicion and distrust toward other people. They believe that others are against them and constantly look for evidence to support their suspicions. They are hostile toward others and react angrily to perceived insults.

Schizoid personality disorder involves social isolation and a lack of desire for close personal relationships. People with this disorder prefer to be alone and seem withdrawn and emotionally detached. They seem indifferent to praise or criticism from other people.

People with schizotypal personality disorder engage in odd thinking, speech, and behaviour. They may ramble or use words and phrases in unusual ways, and they may believe they have magical control over others. They feel very uncomfortable with close personal relationships and tend to be suspicious of others. Some research suggests this disorder is a less severe form of schizophrenia.

Many psychiatrists and psychologists use two additional diagnoses. Depressive personality disorder is characterized by chronic pessimism, gloominess, and cheerlessness. In passive-aggressive personality disorder, a person passively resists completing tasks and chores, criticizes and scorns authority figures, and seems negative and sullen.

Personality disorders result from a complex interaction of inherited traits and life experience, not from a single cause. For example, some cases of antisocial personality disorder may result from a combination of a genetic predisposition to impulsiveness and violence, very inconsistent or erratic parenting, and a harsh environment that discourages feelings of empathy and warmth but rewards exploitation and aggressiveness. Borderline personality disorder may result from a genetic predisposition to impulsiveness and emotional instability combined with parental neglect, intense marital conflicts between parents, and repeated episodes of severe emotional or sexual abuse. Dependent personality disorder may result from genetically based anxiety, an inhibited temperament, and overly protective, clinging, or neglectful parenting.

The pervasive and chronic nature of personality disorders makes them difficult to treat. People with these disorders often fail to recognize that their personality has contributed to their social, occupational, and personal problems. They may not think they have any real problems despite a history of drug abuse, failed relationships, and irregular employment. Thus, therapists must first focus on helping the person understand and become aware of the significance of their personality traits.

People with personality disorders sometimes feel that they can never change their dysfunctional behaviour because they have always acted the same way. Although personality change is exceedingly difficult, sometimes people can change the most dysfunctional aspects of their feelings and behaviour.

Therapists use a variety of methods to treat personality disorders, depending on the specific disorder. For example, cognitive and behavioural techniques, such as role playing and logical argument, may help alter a person's irrational perceptions and assumptions about himself or herself. Certain psychoactive drugs may help control feelings of anxiety, depression, or severe distortions of thought. Psychotherapy may help people to understand the impact of experiences and relationships during childhood.

Psychotherapy is usually ineffective for people with antisocial personality disorder because these individuals tend to be manipulative, unreliable, and dishonest with the therapist. Therefore, most mental health professionals favour removing people with this disorder from their current living situation and placing them in a residential treatment centre. Such residential programs strictly supervise patients' behaviour and impose rigid, consistent rules and responsibilities. These programs appear to help some people, but it is unclear how long their beneficial effects last.

Therapists treating people with borderline personality disorder sometimes use a technique called dialectical behaviour therapy. In this type of therapy, the therapist initially focusses on reducing suicidal tendencies and other behaviours that disrupt treatment. The therapist then helps the person develop skills to cope with anger and self-destructive impulses. In addition, the person learns to achieve personal strength through an acceptance of the many disappointments and interpersonal conflicts that are a natural part of life.

Just the same, and in more generalized terminology, such that in these patients there was an alternating expression of complementary sides of a conflict; such as the acting out of the impulse at some times and of the specific defensive character formation or counterphobia reactions against that impulse at other times. While the patients were conscious of these severe contradictions with a bland denial of the implications of this contradiction, and they would also show what appeared to be from the outside a striking lack of concern over this 'compartmentalization' of the mind.

It has to be pointed out that these observations do not seem to fit with what we conceptualize as the defensive operations of 'isolation' and 'denial.' In isolation, it is the specific affect which is kept separate from the ideational representation of the impulse, and these two do not appear in consciousness together. There is a complete, simultaneous awareness of an impulse and its ideational representation in the ego. What are completely separate from each other are complex psychic manifestations, involving affect, ideational content, subjective and behavioural manifestations? In denial, there is a tendency to eliminate from consciousness a sector of the external subjective reality, a sector which appears in contradiction to what the synthesizing function of the ego dictates as ego syntonic. By contrast, there exists what we might call mutual denial of independent sectors of the psychic life. Actually, we might say that there exists alternating 'ego states' (as a way of describing these repetitive, temporarily ego syntonic, compartmentalized psychic manifestations.)

There is no doubt that this state of affairs represents an ego weakness, but it also shows itself as a most rigid kind of structure. As the ego in psychoanalysis, is the term denoting the central part of the personality structure that deals with reality and is influenced by social forces. According to the psychoanalytic theories developed by Sigmund Freud, the ego constitutes one of the three basic provinces of the mind, the other two being the id and the superego. Formation of the ego begins at birth in the first encounters with the external world of people and things. The ego learns to modify behaviour by controlling those impulses that are socially unacceptable. Its role is that of mediator between unconscious impulses and acquired social and personal standards.

In philosophy, ego means the conscious self or 'I.' It was viewed by some philosophers, notably the 17th-century Frenchman René Descartes and the 18th-century German Johann Gottlieb Fichte, as the sole basis of reality; they saw the universe as existing only in the individual's knowledge and experience of it. Other philosophers, such as the 18th-century German Immanuel Kant, proposed two forms of ego, one perceiving and the other thinking. To whether the alternating activation of contradictory ego states might not reflect specific defensive organization, perhaps characteristic of borderline patients, Freud's (1927, 1940) comment on splitting of the ego as a defensive operation, and Fairbairn's (1952) analysis of splitting as a characteristic and crucial defensive operation in schizoid personalities appear to be of special interest in this connexion.

Freud (1940) mentioned in his paper 'Splitting of the Ego in the Process of Defence' the case of a child who solved his conflict by alternately enacting opposite reactions, representing on the one hand his awareness and consideration of reality, and on the other, his unwillingness to accept reality. Freud commented that this 'success' was achieved at the expense of a rupture in the ego that would no t cure but would enlarge, and he added that these two opposite reactions to the conflict remained as the nuclei of this split in the ego. In the 'Outline of Psycho-Analysis,' Freud (1940) stated that splitting of the ego may represent a general development in the psychoses and other psychopathological conditions, among which he mentioned fetishism. He defined splitting of the ego as the coexistence of two contradictory dispositions throughout life (implicitly, conscious ones) which did not influence each other.

Having, in turn, that the observation that each of these mutually unacceptable, 'split' ego states represented a specific transference disposition of the patient of a rather striking kind. It was as if each of these ego states represented a full-fledged transference paradigm, a highly developed, regressive transference reaction in which a specific internalized object relationship was activate in the transference.

It incidentally is assumed, that these phenomena appeared with quite impressive regularity, and that one might actually describe the difference between the typically neurotic and the borderline personality organizations in something like the following terms: In neurotic patients, the unfolding of internalized object relationships in the transference occurs gradually, as regression develops, and as the secondary autonomy of character structure dissolves in actualized transference paradigms. For example, 'depersonified' superego structure (Hartmann and Loewenstein, 1962; Jacobson, 1964) gradually crystalize into specific internalized parental objects. In borderline patients, by contrast, the highest level depersonified superego structure and autonomous ego structure, are missing, and early, conflict-laden object relationships are activated prematurely. In the transference in connexion with ego states that are split off from each other. The chaotic transference manifestations that the borderline patients of these ego states, representing 'non-metabolized' internalized object relations.

The examining as to the transference implications of the contradictory ego states, particularly in the patient are found the premature intensities of the transference feelings, their explosive, rapidity shifting nature, and the lack of impulse control in regard to these affects in the transference in the weakening of his reality testing in connexion with these feelings, are all typically borderline characteristics. Characteristics, as these tend to give the therapeutic situation a chaotic nature, but as one's knowledge increases such circumstances specific to transference can be detected.

Nonetheless, in more general terms, are the defensive functions as occurring to the splitting of the ego, precisely consisting in keeping contradictory, primitive affective states separated from each other, but not the affective states alone: These contradictory affects were inseparably linked with corresponding internalization, and pathological object relations, however, that whatever the origin of this predisposition for splits in the ego to occur, splitting of the ego was a defensive mechanism attempting to deal with early, pathological object relationships. Also, that the persistence of these internalized object relationships is a rather 'non-metabolized' condition within the psychic apparatus and might be a consequence of the splitting operations.

Fairbairn's (1952) analysis of splitting appeared to be of special interest at this point because he had observed the phenomena in patients displaying schizoid tendencies which usually fall into the 'borderline' field. He stated:

> In a word 'impulses' cannot be considered apart from the endopsychic structures which they energize and the object-relationships which they enable these structures to establish; and, equally, 'instincts' cannot profitably be considered as anything more than forms of energy which constitute the dynamic of such endopsychic structures.

Sutherland (1963) in summarizing Fairbairn's formulation, states:

> Such a split involves a division of the pristine ego into structures each of which contain (I) a part of the ego, (ii) the object that characterizes the related relationships, and (iii) the affect of the latter.

In that some important differences between Fairbairn's formulations and those maintained by others will become clear, his observations provide a fertile background for the structural model of internalization of object relations that, perhaps, had to do with the origin of splitting, the predisposition of the ego toward this defensive operation, the relationship between splitting as on the one hand and other defensive operations—especially repression—on the other, and the relationship between the split-off ego states and the more generalized mechanisms of introjection and identification. Actually, these 'non-metabolized' ego states, with a self-image component, an object-image component, and both of these components linked with an early affect, were the pathologically fixed remnants of the normal processes of early introjection.

Furthermore, a tentative model linking the mechanisms of internalization of object relationships on the one hand, with the vicissitudes of instinctual drive derivatives, and of ego formation, on the other. The main propositional suggestions are:

(1) Introjection, identification, and ego identity are three levels of the process of internalization of object relationships in the psychic apparatus; all three will be referred to comprehensively as identification systems. All these processes of internalization bring about psychic precipitates or structures for which we will use exactly the same term as for the respective mechanism. Introjection, for example, will be considered to be both a process of the psychic apparatus and, as a result of that process, a structure.

(2) All these processes of internalization constitute of three basic components, (I) object-images or object representations, (ii) self-images or self-representations, and (iii) drive derivative or dispositions to specified affective states.

(3) Organization of identification systems takes place first at a base level of ego functioning in which splitting is the crucial mechanism for the defensive organization of the ego. Later, an advanced level of defensive organization of the ego is reached, at which repression replaces splitting as the central mechanism.

(4) The degree of ego integration and ego development, and that of superego integration and development, depends on the degree to which repression and allied mechanisms have replaced splitting and allied mechanisms.

Incidently, the concept of introjection as to imply that it is an early, crucial mechanism of development of the ego, and is in regard somewhat related to Klein's (1946) formulation of introjection.

Klein, however, throughout her writings, shifts the meaning of that term, nonetheless, ending with a broad, puzzling comprehensive concept. Also, Heimann (1966) points out, and Klein sees introjection as a consequence of the mode of oral incorporation, or an id-derived metabolic principle. Considerable favour is inclined to introjection as independent psychic structures, mainly growing out of primary autonomous functions (perception and memory) as they are linked with early object relationships, and although introjection will be seen as strongly influenced by oral conflict, they will not be seen as growing out of them.

Menninger and his colleagues' (1963) conception of mental illness as a unitary process, and of the different forms of psychopathology as related to specific orders or levels of defensive organization, stimulated the present effort to clarify two levels of defensive organization of the ego. His and Mayman's (1956) description of periodic ego rupture as a specific order of dyscontrol used for defensive purposes and defining one level of mental illness is relevant to the present analysis: There are clinical forms of the mechanism of splitting which may appear as episodic dyscontrol. Menninger (1963) describes the occurrence of chronic, repetitive aggressive behaviour and episodic impulsive violence, and states that:

> The functional episodic dyscontrol, acute or chronic, is presumed to be the adverting of great failure, a more catastrophic disintegration.

They stress the dynamic importance of severe aggression and paranoid mechanisms and denial as underlying this condition.

Glover's (1956) hypothesis of a multinuclear primitive ego structure, the partial autonomy of ego nuclei in the earliest phases, and the decisive influence of the original state of nucleation of the ego on its later strength analysis of development during the first year of life.

# INTROJECTION, IDENTIFICATION, EGO IDENTITY

The implication as taken through or by the borderline patient who shifted between contradictory ego states, such that these ego states represented, an affect, with a certain object-image or self-representation of the patient while in that affective state represented a 'non-metabolized' internalized object relationship, which in the neurotic patient would develop only over a period of time out of the depersonified ego and superego structures, while in the borderline patient such object relations in a relatively free state were available from very early in the treatment. And, also implies that in all these patients (neurotics, character disorders and borderline personality organizations) eventually the same kind of 'units' can be found, namely internalized early object-relationships represented by a certain affect, object-representation. And self-representation. Even, in rather regressed patients whose rapidly shifting transference dispositions tend to give the therapeutic situation a chaotic nature, these 'units' of affective state, object-representation and self-representation can be seen in the transference. It was this kind of observation which led to conceptualize all processes of internalization of them. The earliest, fully developed interjections probably represented these units in the purest form and thus implied a relatively simple affect, object-image, self-image linked together.

Introjection is the earliest, most primitive and basic level in the organization of internalization reproduction and fixation of an interaction with the environment by means of an organized cluster of memory traces, implying, at least three components: (1) image of an object, (2) the image of the self an interaction with that object, (3) the affective colouring of both the object-image and the self-image under the influence of the drive representative present at the time of the interaction. This process is a mechanism of growth of the psychic apparatus and it is also used for defensive purposes of the ego. Introjection, then, depends of perception and memory (that is, on apparatuses of primary autonomy), but it transcends these and only be a complex and specific organization of perceptions and memory traces but also by linking 'external' perception with the perception of primitive affect states representing drive derivatives.

In the earliest introjection, object and self-image are not yet differentiated from each other (Jacobson, 1964), and the definition of introjection differentiations, refusion, and redifferentiations of the self and object-images have finally crystallized into clearly delimited components. The 'reciprocal smiling response' and Spitz (1965) has described at around three months of age, and considered an indicator of the first organizer of the psyche, probably corresponds to this crystallization.

The affective colouration of the introjection is an essential aspect of it and represents the active valence of introjection, which determines the fusion and organizations of introjection of similar valences. Thus, introjection taking place under the positive valence of libidinal instinctual gratification, as in loving mother-child contact, tend to fuse and become organized in what has been called somewhat loosely, but pregnantly, 'the good internal object.' Introjections take place under the negative valence introjections become organized in the 'bad internal objects.'

In the process of the fusion of introjections with similar valence, homologous components of introjection tend to fuse, self-images with other self-images and object-image with other object-images. Wherefore, this fusion, to a greater extent elaborates greatly upon self-images and object-images as being 'mapped out,' this process contributes to the differentiation of self and object and in the delimitation of ego boundaries. This in turn, significantly organizes and integrates the apparatuses of perception and memory. Thus, later introjections contain an ever growing plexuity of information about the object and the self in any particular interaction.

Even so, identification is a higher-level form of introjection which can only take place when perceptive and cognitive abilities of the child have increased to the point of recognizing the role aspects of interpersonal interaction. Role implies, of which the presence of a socially recognized function that is being carried out by the object or by both participants in the interaction. For example, mother does something with the child (such as helping it to get dressed) yet, that is not only a specific interaction but also actualizes in a certain way the socially accepted role of mother (giving clothes, protecting, teaching), Also the affective component of identification is of a more elaborate and modified character in that this characteristic of introjection as moderating the effects of various developing ego apparatuses and the decrease in splitting mechanisms.

The psychic derivatives of drives, as they enter upon the object relations, are integrated into identifications as well as into introjection, and on more general terms, it is suggested, that the original penetration of the psychic apparatus with drive derivatives is achieved through these internalization processes. The cluster of memory traces implicit in identification comprises as of: (1) the image of an object adopting a role in an interaction with the self, (2) the image of the self more clearly differentiated from the object than in the case of introjection (and possibly playing a complementary role) and (3) an affective colouration of the interaction of a more differentiated, less intense and less diffuse quality than in the case of introjection. Identification is also considered to be a mechanism of growth and the psychic apparatus which may be used for defensive purpose, and intensifications fuse in a way similar to introjection. Actually, introjection form the core of similar, related identifications.

This, however, is a very complex development, because while object relations are continuously internalized (such internalization takes place at gradually higher, more differentiating levels), at the same time the internalized object relations are also 'depersonified' (Jacobson, 1964) and integrate into higher level ego and superego structures such as the ego ideal, character constellations, and autonomous ego functions. Simultaneously with these processes of internalization and depersonification, internal object relations are also organized into persistent object-images which come to represent internally the external world as experienced by the developing ego, which corresponds roughly to what Sandler and Rosenblatt (1962) have called the 'representational world.' It has to be stressed, nonetheless, that this internal world of objects such as seen in conscious, preconscious and conscious fantasies never reproduces the actual world of real people with whom the individual has establishes relationships in the past and the present: It is at most, an approximation, always s strongly influenced by the very early object images of introjections and identifications. It should be stressed also that the 'world of inner objects' as used by Klein, which gives the impressions of remaining as free floating object images in the psychic apparatuses, rather than being related to any specific structures, does not do justice to the plexuity of integration of object relations. Organization of object images takes place both in the sector of depersonified ego structures and in the sector of developing ego identify. Such object images which remain relatively unmodified in the repressed unconscious are less affected by structuralization; in this sense are the primitive, distorted object images that do certainly continue to exist in the unconscious mind. Still, by far the greater part of internalized object images is normally integrates into higher level structures, and those which remain as object representations experience important modifications over the years under the influence of ego growth and later object relationships. The normal outcome of identity formation is that identifications, in which only those aspects of object relations are internalized which are in harmony with the individual identity formation (Ticho). Actually, the enrichment of one's personal life by the internal presence of such selective, partial identifications, representing people who are loved and admired in a realistic way without indiscriminate internalization, constitutes a major source of emotional depth and well being. The normal process of individualization is marked by the shift from identifications to partial, sublimated identifications under the influence of a well-integrated ego identity. One might say that depersonification of internalized object relations, reshaping of part of them so that they come to resemble more the real objects, and individualization are closely related processes (Ticho).

The world of inner objects, then, gradually changes and comes closer to the 'external' perceptions of the reality of significant objects throughout childhood and later life, without ever becoming an actual copy of the environmental world. 'Confirmation,' intrapsychically speaking, is the ongoing process of reshaping the world of inner objects under the influence of the 'reality principle,' of ego maturation and development. And through cycles of projection and introjection.

The persistence of 'non-metabolized' early introjections is the outcome of a pathological fixation of severely disturbed, early object relationships, a fixation which is intimately related to the pathological development of splitting which interferes with the integration of self and object images, and the personification of internalized object relationships is general are under these pathological circumstances, early, non-integrated object images come to the surface; but even then, as is being stressed throughout as we never do have 'free floating' internal objects but are always confronted with the specific ego structures into which they have crystallized.

Keeping in mind our reservations about the concept of the 'Representational world' as a close reproduction of the external world of objects, we might say that ego identity is the highest level organization of the world of object relations in the broadest sense, and comprises the concept of the representational world on the one hand, and that of the self on the other.

## EARLY STAGES OF EGO DEVELOPMENT

Several authors (e.g., Brierley, 1937; Rapaport, 1954, 1960) have stressed the many difficulties in clarifying this issue. For our purpose, what is important is the intense, overwhelming nature of early affect and its irradiating effect on all other perceptual elements of the introjection, so that intense 'negative' affect states related to aggressive drive derivatives create perceptual constellations entirely different from intense 'positive' affect states under the influence of libidinal striving, in externally not too different circumstances. This overwhelming nature of early affective states is the cause of the valence of the introjection of early affective states and is the cause of the valence of the introjection and of the kind of fusion and organization which will take place involving it. 'Positive' and 'negative' introjection, that is, introjections with positive valence and negative valence respectfully, are thus kept completely apart. They are kept apart at first simply because they happen separately and because of the lack of capacity of the ego for integration of introjection and activated by similar valences, but then gradually in response to anxiety, because of the ego's active use of this separation for defensive purposes. This is actually the origin of splitting as a mechanism of defence.

Introjection, the earliest form of identification systems, may be considered as precipitants around which ego nuclei consolidate. It is suggested that fusion of similar positive introjections constitute such ego nuclei and that they have an essential function in directing the organization of perception, memory, and indirectly that of other autonomous ego functions, such as those outlined by Murphy (1963): The general level of psychomotor activity, control over delay; orientation and planning of activities; flexibility in shifting attention differentiation of all kind of stimuli, and integration of experience and action (skill).

At what point does the ego come into existence? Certain ego structures, and functions connected with them, existed from the beginning of life: Perception, the capacity to establish memory traces, and the other functions just mentioned. These are essentially functions of the primary autonomous apparatuses (Hartmann, 1939). On the other hand, the capacity to establish introjections represents a higher level of inborn capacity, intimately linked with the 'perceptualization' of drive derivatives.

It is suggested that the ego as a differentiated psychic structure, in the sense of Freud's (1923) description, come about at the point when introjections are used for defensive purposes, specifically in an early defensive organization against overwhelming anxiety. We could describe a state, briefly as it may be, 'forerunners of the ego,' a stage during which a sufficient development and organization of introjections has to take place in order for these defensive operations to function. As stated, introjection with positive valence under the influence of libidinal striving are built up separately from introjections with negative valence under the influence of aggressive striving. What originally was a lack of integrative capacity, in the presence of overwhelming anxiety, is gradually used defensively by the emerging ego and maintains introjections with different valences dissociated or split from each other. This serves the purpose of preventing the generalization of anxiety throughout the ego from the foci of negative introjection and protects the integration of positive introjection into a primitive ego centre.

The first ego state probably one in which the 'good internal objects' (the early positive introjections with mostly undifferentiated and fused self and object images) and the 'good external objects' (such reality aspects of external objects which are really 'part-objects') constitute the earliest defensive organization of the ego (the 'purified pleasure ego') while all negative introjections are 'ejected' (Jacobson, 1964) and considered as 'not me.' One might also say that by the act of this ejection, 'me' is established.

Later, under the influence of maturing perception, motor control and from the internal psychic world, a typical tripartite situation exists, as (1) the ego is organized around the positive introjections ('good internal object'), (2) a positive, libido-invested aspect of reality is acknowledged as 'external reality' in intimate relation with the ego, and (3) an entity of 'bad external objects,' representing both realistically frustrating or threatening external objects and the projected negative early introjections, complete the picture.

This active separation by the ego of positive and negative introjections, which implies a complete division of the ego and, as a consequence, of external reality as well, is in essence, the defensive mechanism of splitting. In the earliest stage of the ego, when active splitting operations start, the ego only presents fused positive introjections within which object and self images are also fused, and early 'positive part-objects.' There is as yet no ego boundary between the positive external part-objects and their mental representations. Negative introjections (within which self and object images, internal and external objects are also fused) are ejected' and active splitting keeps them purified pleasure ego dissociated from the 'not me.' A t the later stage which reality is more acknowledged by the ego, both in the awareness of the difference between good external 'part-objects' and good internal objects, and in the growing separation within the ego of object and self images. This stage also implies the beginning delimitations of ego boundaries in the area of positive object relaxation, the beginning of reality testing. Splitting is now maximally present and permits the complete projection of negative introjections ('bad internal objects') onto the outside. Introjection is now also used as a defensive mechanism in that an intensification of positive interactions, the development of dependent striving, takes place not only in relation to libidinal drive derivatives but also as a protection against anxiety and helplessness, especially when these are increased by the fear of projected bad external objects. Spitz's (1965) description of the; eight-month anxiety' that appears when the child is approached by a stranger, explains this reaction as a consequence of the infant's now being active to differentiate his mother from other people and the infant's interpreting the situation as an indication that

## Object Relations Theory

mother has left him. It may well be that this specific anxiety is also relates to the mechanism of splitting, to the defensive use of mother's; good' image as a protection against fear of (projected) bad external objects, the 'stranger.'

Splitting as an active defensive process can come into existence only after introjections have fully developed. Splitting processes probably develop around the third and fourth month of life, reach a maximum over the next few months, and gradually disappear in the latter part of the first year.

In summary, the maturation and development of primary ego apparatuses gives origin, at one point, to introjections, which in turn become an essential organizer of what is going to be the ego as an integrated structure, after some development of introjections as psychic structures, a point is reached when introjections are actively kept apart or split for defensive purposes, at which point a centralizing, synthetic ego function (synthetic in the sense of overall organizational purpose) has come into existence and, with it, the ego as a definite organizational structure. Thus, introjection, the earliest point of convergence of object relationships and instinctual drive representatives, may be visualized as an essential 'switch' bringing the ego into operational readiness. Late r developments of all ego structures which we have call, identification systems, which in turn determine later on a higher level ego organizer; namely, ego identity. At that later point ego identity takes over the highest level of the ego's synthetic functions.

The mechanism of splitting may be considered an outgrowth of what was a primarily 'physiological' lack of integrative capacity of the psychic apparatus. It becomes an essential defensive operation of the early ego, and splitting in this regard is splitting of the globular, poorly differentiated ego. Later on, however, splitting becomes a mechanism especially involved in the organization and in the pathology of identification system. The object relations determined structures of the ego (that is, the self, the representational world, and ego identity in general). In these later stages of development, the integrity of the ego of less interfered with by splitting mechanisms, secondary autonomy is partially maintained even with severe regression and with splitting of the self and representational world. By contrast, excessive, pathological early splitting threatens the integrity of the ego at that point and also the future developmental capacity of the ego as a whole. It has to be stressed that in the active keeping apart of introjections of opposite valence, what is split is not only affect states of the ego but also object images and self images. Excessive pathological splitting therefore interferes not only with the integration of affects, but also with integration of the self and the development of the representational world. Because of the fundamental importance of early introjections in the organization and integration of the ego as a whole, pathological splitting carries over into splitting of the ego as an organization.

The present model of early ego development is based on Hartmann's (1939, 1950) assumption of an undifferentiated phase of development, a common matrix to the ego and the id; It specifies a certain stage in which the ego may be considered for the first time as an integrated structure, although of course, oscillations back and forth from that point have to be assumed. Object relationships are seen as an essential ego organizer, even much earlier than the time in which self and objects are differentiated. Our model implies a disagreement with the object-relationships orientation of Fairbairn (1952) and Melanie Klein (Heimann, 1943-44; Klein, 1952). Their assumption that an ego exists from birth. As mentioned, introjection is not seen as derived from oral incorporative fantasies, but from primary autonomous apparatuses of perception and memory. Here Fairbairn's criticism of Klein is relevant:

> Mclanie Klein has never satisfactorily explained how fantasies of incorporating objects orally can give rise to the establishment of internal objects as endopsychic structures—and, unless they are such structures, they cannot be mere figments of fantasy.

Jacobson's (1964) criticism of Klein's lack of differention of self-images from object images in her concept of inner objects. The assumption that inner reality can be differentiated from outer reality from the beginning of life is clearly rejected by our model. With all these reservations, the agreeing with Klein's (1952) formation that the drive toward integration and synthesis, the establishment of defences against anxiety, the development of processes of introjection and projection, the development of object relations and the mechanism of splitting are all essential conditions for the ego to come into full operation.

## LATER STAGES OF STRUCTURAL DEVELOPMENT

The next stage in normal development is crucial one for this period of awkward adjustments. The maturation of autonomous ego apparatuses, the delimitation of ego boundaries, and the gradual development of higher forms of introjection (identifications) in the area of positive object relations, make splitting become more difficult because the reality of 'negative' interaction and their 'contamination' of purely positive introjection can no longer be eliminated and kept from the synthetic processes of the ego. Sometimes, though the environment may actually reinforce splitting mechanisms, given certain types of pathology in the paternal figures. Normally, at a certain point, the stage is reached in which the synthetic processes bring positive and negative introjections and identifications together and a radically new situation develops.

At this point, the positive self-images of positive introjections are connected with the negative introjections, and the positive object-images are the same as connected with the respective negative object-images. At the same time the negative, aggressive determined affects and the positive, libidinal determined affects are also brought together, and a typical situation arises which probably corresponds to what Klein (1939, 1940) has described as the 'depressive position.' Tension between different contradictory self-images or self-images develop, with the appearance of guilt and concern (Winnicott, 1955) because of the acknowledged aggression of the self toward the object which appeared to be bad before and is now seen as part of a 'total object' which is both good and bad. Built, concern and mourning over the good object, which is felt partly lost by this synthesized integration and partly endangered, are new affective dispositions which strongly develop in the ego at this stage (Winnicott, 1955),

The fusion of positive and negative introjections implies a fusion of their affect components, and with this a modulation of these affects. The irradiating effect of purely positive and purely negative affective states diminishes, and the mutual copenetration of libidinal and aggressive drive derivatives fosters a broader spectrum of affect dispositions of the ego. This development, essential for normal psychic growth, also triggers off an additional development of the intrapsychic life: The development of the image of an ideal self representing the striving for reparation of guilt and for the re-establishment of an ideal., positive relationship, between the self and object. the image of an ideal object which represents the unharmed, all-loving, all-forgiving object completes the picture (Jacobson, 1964; Sandler, 1963).

Anxiety constitutes a basic motive for defensive operations of the ego at all levels of development. Guilt feelings, an ego state brought under the influence of fusion of identification systems with opposite valence and the real-self/ideal-self tensions which originate in this process. Later become the typical motive of defence prompted by superego demands. In other words, the superego uses the capacity of the ego for experiencing guilt for its own purposes.

The fusion of positive with negative introjections takes place respectively in different degrees of success in the fusion depending on the different areas. There exists a tendency to fusion and defusion of positive and negative introjections, in the course of which regression to earlier states with strong splitting and progression to higher synthesized ones, reflects reality testing and the work of the synthetic function of the ego (Nunberg, 1955) at the level of the self and internal objects. While this fusion takes place at the levels of early introjections as well as later ones, it is probably that it reaches its definite crystallization into a new 'four unit system' composed of object, self, ideal object and ideal self, only with later identification systems.

From here on, synthetic processes show an accelerated development: integrative processes combining all kinds of introjections and identifications onto the ego identity take place, and this expands and solidifies all structures of the ego. Further delimitation of ego boundaries occur, there is further development of the ego's centralized control over perception and motility, and 'pockets' of intolerable severely negative introjections and dissociated from the ego nucleus or core (Fairbairn) and lose their previous free access to perception and motility; from now on, negative introjections may be directed repressed.

It is suggested that this consolidation of the ego establishes repression as a new central defensive operation in contrast to the splitting of the earlier ego. In fact, this developmental step brings about a fundamental difference between early and later ego development, however, discussions of splitting and repression as two basic mechanisms of ego defence at different levels of development, and the energic conditions related to this change will return.

The continuing processes of introjection and projection now also permit the internalization of previously feared, dangerous, frustrating objects (especially prohibitive parental images); and fusion takes place between these introjected prohibitive parental images and the guilt determined. As ideal objects which were mentioned, however, the product of this fusion is partly integrated into the ego and partly repressed, and these nuclei of fused ideal-object/prohibitive parental images constitute forerunners of the superego. Fusion between the ideal self and the ideal objects come to constitute the ego ideal (Jacobson, 1964), again, part of which is integrated into the ego and part of which is repressed and synthesized as other forerunners of the superego and later contributes with them to the definite formation of the superego.

From this point onward, a change in the patterns of growth of the ego through the development and nuclei of identification systems occur, that drive derivatives now entering the psychic apparatus are partially repressed before they enter the ego nucleus and become directly part of the rejected, unacceptable identification systems which constitute the dynamic unconscious in its definite form. On the one hand, intense guilt feelings, derived from the tensions between self and ideal self, and from the 'prohibitive-parent/ideal-object' pressures on the ego, may be projected onto the outside and reintrojected directly into the superego. Guilt is projected in the form of accusations or threats attributed to parental figures, and this projection determine in the reinforcement of introjection of prohibitive parental images into the superego.

The next step is the fusion of the superego nuclei and the development of an organized superego which gradually becomes abstracted and 'depersonified.' we refer too the comprehensive analysis of Jacobson (1964), who has described how the superego is integrated and systematized, incorporating early forerunners derived from archaic, projected and reintrojected object images, the major aspect of the ego ideal, and the later internalization of more realistic parental prohibitions and demands. Hartmann and Loewenstein's (1962) and Sandler's (1960) analysis is also relevant here.

A tentative consideration on timing may be of interest at this point. All these processes take place over the first two or three years of life, and certainly do not crystallize in the first six months. In suggesting that splitting as an active mechanism comes into operation probably around the third month of life, and reaches its maximum several months later, only gradually disappearing in the latter part of the first year. The later developments of the ego that have been described, and which presuppose an overcoming to an important degree of splitting processes, cannot crystallize earlier than in the second and third years of life. Superego formation is a later and more complex structure-building process than early ego formation. Although it would be essentially its phase of a late classical theory, and would, if, only to suggest, that its main components are built up during the second and third year. Such is the close relationship between higher-level ego structures, as the ideal self, the ideal object, and the intimately connected ego ideal, on the one hand, and the formation of superego components on the other. The definite integration of all the superego components probably takes place mainly between the fourth and sixth year, and depersonification and abstraction of the superego become quantitatively significant between the fifth and seventh years. Jacobson (1964) has pointed out that even under ideal circumstances superego integration is not completely accomplished by that time.

One consequence of this model of structural development of the psychic apparatus is the conceptualization of the dynamic unconscious as a system composed of rejected introjection and identification systems. In other words, the repressed portion of the id would posses an internal organization, and specific structures composed of self-image, object-image, and unacceptable impulse components. One might visualize displacement, condensation and other primary process operations as the result of 'temporary circuits' on the id linking different repressed identifications systems on each other under the guiding principle of a common affective valence. A related conceptualization has been suggested by van der Waals (1952) who ended his discussion at the 1951 symposium on the mutual influence in the development of ego and id, saying:

> We would have to conclude that the repressed portion of the id is not pure id, but an ego id, just like the undifferentiated phases in the early part of psychic life.

Again, in suggesting that both libido and aggression make their appearance in the psychic apparatus as part of early introjection, and this are intimately connected to the object relationship in the context of definite early ego structures.

## SPLITTING AND REPRESSION AS CENTRAL MECHANISMS

In contrast, splitting and repression function as defensive operations; Freud (1915) stated that:

> . . . the essence of repression lies simply in turning something away, and keeping it at a distance from the conscious.

Anna Freud (1936) states, in a comment on Freud's (1926) reference to repression in 'Inhibitions. Symptoms and Anxiety,'

> Repression consists in the withholding or expulsion of an idea or affect from the conscious ego. It is meaningless to speak of repression where the ego is still merged with the id.

It is true of course, that when repression is combined with other mechanisms as for instance, with isolation in the case of obsessive-compulsive symptom formation, the ideational content of what is repressed may become conscious, but the impulse continues to be kept outside consciousness. In fact, intellectualization, isolation, displacement, and also what we would refer to as 'higher-level' character defences (especially reaction formations and inhibitory types of character traits), drive derivatives in the form of specific affects and the ideational representation of the respective impulse do not appear in consciousness together. The complete simultaneous awareness of an impulse and its respective ideational representation are kept out of the ego (Madison, 1961). By contrast, complete consciousness of the impulse, it is suggested, may exist at a 'lower level' of characterlogical defences, such as those seen in severe 'acting out' and impulse-ridden characters and in the defences characteristic of borderline personality structures (such as early forms of projection and especially projective identification [Rosenfeld, 1963] and denial) all of which are closely related to splitting (Segal, 1964).

Splitting, it has been suggested is to be a mechanistic characteristic of the first stages of development of the ego. It grows out of the naturally occurring lack of integration of the first introjections, and is then used defensively in order to protect the positive introjection (good internal objects) and thus indirectly fosters ego growth. Splitting as a defensive mechanism consists in the dissociation or active maintaining apart of identification systems with opposite valence, that is, conflicting identification systems, without regard to the access to consciousness and to perceptual or motor control. The drive derivative attains full emotional, ideational and motor consciousness, but is completely separate from other segments of the conscious psychic experience. In other terms, in the process of splitting, the ego protects itself against anxiety connected with early intrapsychic conflicts (represented by conflicts between introjections of opposite valences) by a regressive nucleation. As stated, splitting is typically a mechanism of the early ego in which identification systems have not crystallized into higher organizations such as the self or the representational world, but it can pathologically that affects the self, and ego identity in general. Hopefully, this clarifies the question whether what is split is the ego or the self. The crucial intervention of the mechanism of splitting occurs at a time at which the self has not, differentiated within the ego, and at that point what is split is the ego. Later on, when the self has consolidated as a definite structure (a substructure of ego identity), what is typically split when excessive use of this mechanism is made (for example, in severe character disorders) is the self and no longer the ego.

Repression, by contrast, is a central defensive mechanism of the ego at a later stage that in which splitting is predominant, and consists in the rejection of an impulse or its ideational representation, or both, from the conscious ego. Similarly to the way in which splitting, at a more primitive level of development, is reinforced by projection, denial, and other typical 'psychotic' defences, repression, or its higher level of ego development, is reinforced by mechanisms such as isolation, displacement, and other typical neurotic defensive operations. Repression consolidates and protects the nucleus or core of the ego, and contributes crucially to the definite delimitation of ego boundaries. At the time when splitting prevailed, and under pathological conditions when this continues to be so over the years, the ego protects itself against anxiety by a defensive nucleation which necessarily implies a serious price to pay in regard to the ego's synthetic functions and reality testing. After repression has become predominant and in the less severe forms of psychopathology (mainly the neuroses and moderate character disorders), the ego protects itself against the anxiety connected with intolerable conflicts by eliminating these conflicts from consciousness. Repression is thus a much more effective defensive operation, but t requires strong countercathexis, because of the blocking of discharge that characterizes repression but not splitting. Repression is a much more adapted and effective defence; but in order for it to become established, important energic preconditions have to be met.

The normal fusion of positive and negative introjections which takes place at the time when repression comes into existence, also implies a fusion of their affect components, and with this a modification of these affects. Actually, it is suggested that neutralization (Hartmann, 1955; Menninger, 1938) takes place quite decisively at this point of combination of libidinal and aggressive affects. The synthesis of identification systems neutralizes aggression., and possible provides the most important single energy source for the higher level of repressive mechanisms to come into operation, and implicitly, for the development of secondary autonomy in general. One consequence of pathological circumstance, in which splitting is excessive, is that this neutralization does not take place or takes place insufficiently, and thus an important energy source for ego growth fails. Splitting, then, is a fundamental cause of ego weakness, and as splitting also requires less countercathexis than repression, a weak ego falls back easily on splitting, and a vicious circle is created by which ego weakness and splitting reinforce each other.

Some clinical applications of this model are seen in some severe character disorders the alternating expression of complementary sides of a conflict, such as the acting out of the impulse at some times and of the specific defensive character formations against that impulse at other times. In that, the patient may be conscious of severe contradictions in his behaviour, but he can alternate between opposite striving with a bland denial of this contradiction and with what appears to be, from the outside, a striking lack of concern over it. The analyst may try to interpret 'directly' the implication of each of the two sides of the conflict as they present themselves, only to realize after some time than what appeared to be a 'working through' of conscious, deep conflicts, really was repetitive, oscillating acting out of that conflict without any intrapsychic change. The conflict is not 'unconscious' in the stricter sens connected with repression, and so long as the rigid barrier between contradictory ego states is maintained the patient is free from anxiety. Only the attempts to bridge these independently expressed, conflicting ego nuclei bring about severe anxiety, mobilize new defensive operations and may bring about changes of splitting as a primary defensive operation which has to be overcome for any further changes to be achieved in such patients, is an important consequence of this formulation for psychotherapeutic techniques.

In some severe character disorders, rather than alternating expressions of complementary sides of the conflict, it is what appears on the surface to be simply lack of impulse control connected with ego weakness which reflects the mechanism of splitting. Such selective 'lack of impulse control' is often of a highly specific kind and represents the emerging into consciousness of a split identification system. It is the very episodic character of this lack of impulse control, the typical ego syntonicity of the impulse being expressed during the time of impulsive behaviour, the complete lack of emotional 'contact' between that part of the patient's personality and the rest of his self experience, and finally, the bland denial secondarily defending the contradictions between his usual feelings and behaviour and his behaviour during the specific episodes, which reflect the presence of strong splitting operations. For example, a patient presented episodic sexual promiscuity, in contrast to her usually rigid, inhibitory puritanical sexual and social life. She showed no lack of impulse control in other areas of her personality. The consistent interpretation of the rigid dissociation between the episodes of sexual promiscuity and her usual self, rather than direct efforts to 'strengthen her impulse control' or to interpret 'deeper meaning' of her acting out (such as unconscious guilt which could effectively be brought to the surface only much later. Proving an effective way of overcoming her pseudo-lack of impulse control. In general, a consistent interpretation of the patient's efforts to keep two areas of his experience completely separated from each other may bring about, for the first time, more deeply felt anxiety and guilt, and may also mobilize the conflict more specifically in the transference.

Actually, a classification of character disorder according to the degree of splitting and to the degree of repressive mechanisms present implicitly in the characterlogical structure, might prove clinically meaningful. We might classify character disorders from a 'low level' extreme, represented by the chaotic and impulse ridden characters in whom splitting tends to be predominant, to the milder 'avoidance trait' character, with the classical reaction formation types of character structures somewhere in the middle.

I would only suggest to designate this broad variety of psychopathology as borderline personality organization rather than borderline states; or simply; borderlines,' because it appears rather that these patients represent no t only acute or chronic transitional states between the neuroses on the one side and the psychoses on the other, But a specific, and remarkable stable form of pathological ego structure, such that one of the main features of ego structure in these cases is the predominance of splitting mechanisms and related defensive operations, with the concomitant failure of the normal processes of development and integration of identification systems. Such a pathological failure of early ego development can occur because of constitutional defect or retardation in the development of the apparatuses of primary autonomy which underlie the operation of introjection and identification processes. In this case, one might say, the non-object-relations determined substructural ego deficiencies of the ego are defective and interfere with the development of internalized object relations. Actually, this state of affairs is probably more characteristic of psychotic states that of borderline personality organizations, and is characterized by regressive fusion of the earliest self and object images and concomitant lack of development of ego boundaries (Jacobson, 1964). More characteristic for the borderline personality organization may be a failure related to a constitutionally determined lack of anxiety tolerance interfering with the phase of synthesis of introjection of opposite valences. The most important cause of failure in the borderline pathology is probably a quantitative predominance of negative introjection. Excessive negative introjections may stem from a constitutionally determined intensity of aggressive drive derivatives and from severe early frustrations. From a clinical point of view, extremely severe aggressive and self-aggressive striving are consistently related to borderline personality organization, and whatever the origin of this aggression, once it operates as part of early introjections, a number of pathological sequences come about hyper cathected

First of all, the painful nature of the object relation under an 'all out' negative valence increases anxiety and the need to project aggression in the form of projection of negative introjections, which then become 'bad external objects.' under these circumstances, splitting is reinforced as a fundamental protection of the positive introjections ('good internal anxiety'), and as a general protection of the ego against diffusion of anxiety. The need to preserve the good internal and outer objects leads not only to excessive splitting, but also to a dangerous 'pre-depressive idealization' (seeing the external object as totally good, in order to make sure that they cannot be contaminated, spoiled, or destroyed b y the projected 'bad external objects'). Pre-depressive idealization creates unrealistic, all-good and powerful object images and later on, a corresponding hyper-cathected, blown up, omnipotent ego ideal which is quite typical of borderline patients. The high degree of projection of aggressive self and object images of the negative introjections perpetuates a dangerous world of persecuting objects, and in short, there are a consequence of excessive splitting, but then, in turn reinforce splitting. Excessive splitting also interferes with the strengthening of ego boundaries because of its interference with fusion of similar introjections, and therefore, with the normal, gradual mapping out of the self and objects. Under the condition of lack of differentiation of ego boundaries, the mechanism of projection remain at a rather primitive, inefficient level, in which of what is projected outside is still in part, confusingly felt inside, with the additional need to exert control over external objects into whom aggression has been projected, all of which is characteristic of 'projective identification' (Kernberg, 1965; Klein, 1946; Rosenfeld, 1963). Projective identification, an early form of projection, is actually a mechanism typically present in patients in whom splitting operations are very strong, and who also present the early form of idealization which we have called 'pre-depressive idealization.'

Later forms of idealization are of a different kind, typically involve a reaction formation against unconscious guilt toward the object, and are protective devices against fear of attack by bad objects. In more general terms, may, perhaps, that the numerous defensive mechanisms change their characteristics with ego development, concomitantly with the shift from predominance of splitting to the predominance of repression.

The pathological state of affairs that, as described in regard to borderline personality organization, also determines the superego pathology typical of these patients. The internalization of unrealistically idealized early object images creates impossible internalized demands: Catastrophic fusions between these unrealistic ideal objects and other superego components, such as threatening, demanding, 'external persecutors,' induce the formation of sadistic superego nuclei which interfere with the normal internalization of more realistic parental prohibitions and demand, and with the integration of the superego itself. One other consequence of all these developments is that both excessive splitting and the lack of superego integration interfere with further synthesis of the ego nucleus or core. Mutual reinforcements of ego weakness and splitting, end up in a pathologically fixated personality organization in which early drive derivatives, as part of split-up ego states, persist dangerously close to consciousness and to directly influencing all aspects of psychic life.

In the attempt sketch briefly, the difference between borderline personality organization on the one hand, and the more normal development of the ego and superego compatible with the development of neurosis and normality of the other. The difference between borderline personality organization and psychotic regression or fixation are another field of investigation which might be illuminated by suggested conceptualization. It is possible that in psychotic reaction the main common psychopathological factor (in addition to persistence of splitting mechanisms) is the lack of differentiation between self and object of those early self and object images under the impact of pathogenic factors which in milder situations induce excessive splitting only. And not refusion of self and object images. Lack of differentiation of self and object images in the earliest introjections interferes with the differentiation between self and object, And, therefore, with the delimitation of ego boundaries. Perhaps, it might be to extend extent primary autonomous ego apparatuses, especially perception and memory, may influence the degree to which self and object images can be differentiated. Quantitative factors involving the degree of aggressive drive derivatives, in the degree of objective deprivation and frustration, and the degree of the early ego's anxiety tolerance, may also be crucially involved.

What is the relationship between the degree to which primary or secondary thought processes predominate, and the degree to which splitting or repressive mechanisms predominate? It may be to suggest, that identification systems night be visualized as precipitates of the ego, around the cognitive functions and adaptive aspects of defensive functions construct a secondary, stable 'interstitial web.' This 'interstitial web' gives strength to the whole ego structure, preserves the delimitation of early object relationships and contributes further to the delimitation of ego boundaries. On a higher level of organization, these interstitial structures then emancipate themselves toward independent structures. We can also can say, that secondary autonomy of thought processes presupposes such emancipation through processes from their connexion with early identification systems. The modification of affective dispositions available to the ego also fosters indirectly the emancipation of thought processes, because the irradiating effect of earlier 'pure' affective states exerts a powerful regressive pull in the direction of primary process thinking, which decreases when modification of affects occurs. The emancipation of cognitive functions, is, of course, always a relative one, but rather severe failure of such an independent development occurs in the borderline personality organization. Under these circumstances, thought processes remain strongly linked to 'non-metabolized' identification systems, abstraction and generalization is interfered with, and regressive pull of 'pure' affective state, influences thought processes. In its end, an insufficient introjection deprives the ego of an important part of the energic factors which permit thought processes to develop secondary autonomy. In general terms, excessive splitting brings about interference with the later differentiation of apparatuses of primary autonomy and with the full development of secondary autonomy. It interferes with the development of the ego nucleus or core as it weakens the concomitant capacity for repression and related defensive operations of the higher level.

# REFERENCES

* Brierley, M. (1937). Affects on theory and practice. In: Trends in Psychoanalysis. (London, Hogarth. 1951.
* Erikson, E. H. (1950) Growth and crises of the healthy personality. In: Identity and the Life Cycle. (New York): Int. Univ, Press, 1959.
  -(1956), The problem of ego identity. ibid.
* Fairbairn, W. D. (1952) Psychoanalytic Studies of the Personality. (Amer. Title: An Object-Relations Theory of the Personality.) (London; Tavistock; New York: Basic Books).
* Freud, A. (1936). The Ego and the Mechanisms of Defence. (London; Hogarth, 1937), New York: Int. Univ. Press, 1946).
* Freud, S. (1915), Repression, S. E. 14.
  -(1923) The Ego and the Id. S. E. 19.
  -(1926). Inhibitions, Symptoms and Anxiety. S. E 20.
  -(1927). Fetishism. S. E. 21.
  -!940a) An Outline of Psycho-analysis. S. E. 23
  -(1940b), Splitting of the ego in the processes of defence. S. E. 23.
* Glover, E. (1956), On the Early Development of Mind, (New York: Int, Univ. Press.)
* Guntrip, H. (1961). Personality Structure and Human Interaction. (London: Hogarth; New York. Int. Univ. Press.)
* Hartmann, H. (1939)., Ego Psychology and the Problem of Adaptation. (New York: Int. Univ. Press, 1958.)
  -(1950) Comment s on the psychoanalytic theory of the ego. In: Essay is on Ego Psychology. (London: Hogarth; New York: Int. Univ. Press, 1964.)
  -(1955). Notes on the theory of sublimation, ibid.
* Hartmann, H. and Loewenstein, R., M. (1962). Note s on the Superego. Psychoanal. Study Child, 17.
* Heimann, P. (1943-44). Certain functions of introjection and projection in early infancy. In. Develops in Psycho-Analysis, ed. Klein et.al. ( London: Hogarth, 1952.)
* Klein, M. (1939). A Contribution to the psychogenesis of manic-depressive states. In: Contribution to Psycho-Analysis. (London: Hogarth. 1950.)
  -(1940). Mourning and its relation to manic-depressive States. Ibid.

- (1946). Notes on some schizoid mechanisms, In: Development in Psychoanalysis ed. Klein et al. (London. Hogarth, 1952.)
- (1952). Discussion of the mutual influence in the development of ego and id. Psychoanal. Study of the Child.
* Knight, R. P. (1954). Borderline States, In: Psychoanalytic Psychiatry and Psychology, ed, Knight and Friedman. (New York. Int. Univ. Press.)
* Madison, F. (1961) Freud's Concept of Repression and Defence. (Minneaolis: Univ, of Minnesota Press.)
* Menninger, K. (1938). Man Against Himself. (New York. Harcourt Brace.)
* Menninger, K. and Mayman, M. (1956). Episodic dyscontrol: order of stress adaptation. Bull. Menninger Clinic 20.
* Menninger, K. Mayman, M. And Pruysder. P. (1963) The Vital Balance. (New Y or k:Viking.)
* Murphy, L. (1963) From a report presented to Topeka Psychoanalytic Institute Research Seminar, Ma y 15, 1963.
* Murphy, L. (1964) Adaptational tasks in childhood in our culture. Bull. Menninger Clinic, 28.
* Nunberg, H. (1955), Principles of Psychoanalysis (New York: Int. Univ. Press.)
* Rapaport, D,. On the psychoanalytic theory of affect s, (1954). In: Psychoanalytic Psychiatry and Psychology, ed. Knight and Friedman. (New York: Int. Univ. Press.)
- (1960). The Structure of Psychoanalytic Theory. (New York: Int. Univ. Press.)
* Rosenfeld, H. (1963). Notes on the psychopathology and psycho-analytic treatment of schizophrenia. In: Psychotic States (London Hogarth, 1965.)
* Sandler, J. (1960). On the concept of the superego: Psychoanal. Study Child, 15.
* Sandler, J. And Rosenblatt. B. (1962). The Concept of the representational world. Psychoanal. Study Child, 17.
* Sandler, J. Holder. A. and Meers. D. (1963). The ego ideal and the ideal self. Psychoanal. Study Child, 18.
* Spitz, R. A. (1965). The First Year of Life. (New York: Int. Univ. Press.)
* Sutherland, J. D. (1963). Object-relations theory and the conceptual model of psychoanalysis. Brit. J. Med. Psychol., 36.

* Van de r Waals, H. G. (1952). Discussion of the mutual influences in the development of ego and id. Psychoanal, Study Child, 7.
* Winnicott, D. W. (1955). The depressive position in normal emotional development. Brit. J. Ned. Psychoanal, anal. 28.

# CHAPTER SEVEN

# The Therapeutic Action of Psychoanalysis

Advances in our understanding of the therapeutic action of psychoanalysis should be based on deeper insight into the psychoanalytic process. By 'psychoanalytic process' is to mean by the significant interactions between patient and analyst which ultimately lead to structural changes in the patent's personality. Today, after more than fifty years of psychoanalytic investigation and practice, we are in a position to appreciate, if not to understand better, the role which interaction with environment plays in the formation, development, and continued integrity of the psychic apparatus. Psychoanalytic ego-psychology, based on a variety of investigations concerned with ego-development, has given us some tools to deal with the central problem of the relationship between the development of psychic structures and interaction with other psychic structures, and of the connexion between ego-formation and object-relations.

If 'structural changes in the patient's personality' means anything, it must mean that we assume that ego-development is resumed in the therapeutic process in psychoanalysis. And this resumption of ego-development is contingent on the relationship with a new object, as the analyst. The nature and the affects of this new relationship are to so extreme a degree to be fruitful to attempt correlations as our understanding of the significance of object-relations for the formation and development of the psychic apparatus with the dynamic of the therapeutic process.

Problems, however, more or less established psychoanalytic theory and tradition concerning object-relations the phenomenon of transference, the relations between instinctual drives and ego, as well as concerning the function of the analyst in the analytic situation, have to be dealt with, yet some therapists have found it unavoidably clarifying as by inactions given to personal opinion. That is to say, in thinking toward or in the emerging of repeatedly forming of the central theme so as to deal with such problems. Therefore, is anything but a systematic presentation of the subject-matter. Moreover, this is, however, not by any measure a result of affective techniques in cement of the psychoanalysis. A better understanding of the therapeutic action of psychoanalysis may lead to changes in technique, but anything such clarification may entail as far as technique is concerned will have to be worked out carefully and is not have in capacity the representational determinants upon which the topic holds.

I

While the fact of object-relationship between patient and analyst is taken for granted, classical formulations concerning therapeutic action and concerning the role of the analyst in the analytic relationship do not reflect our present understanding of the dynamic organization of the psychic apparatus, in that of modern psychoanalysis ego-psychology represents far more than an addition to the psychoanalytic theory of instinctual drives. In other words, it is the elaboration of a more comprehensive theory of the dynamic organization of the psychic apparatus, and psychoanalysis is the process of integrating our knowledge of instinctual drives, gained during earlier stages of its history, into such a psychological theory. The impact of psychoanalytic ego-psychology has on the development of psychoanalysis indicated that ego-psychology is not concerned with just another part of the psychic apparatus, but in giving a new dimension to the conception of the psychic apparatus as a whole.

In an analysis, we have opportunities to observe and investigate primitive as well as more advanced interaction-processes, that is, interactions between patient and analyst which lead to or form steps in ego-integration and disintegration. Such interactions, which are called integrative (and disintegrative) experiences, occur many times but do not often as such become the focus of our attention and observation, and unnoticed. Apart from the difficulty for the analyst of self observation while in interaction with his patient, there seems to be a specific reason stemming from theoretical bias when such interactions not go unnoticed but frequently are denied. The theoretical given a bias to is the view of the psychic apparatus as a closed system. Thus the analyst is seen, not as a co-actor on the analytic stage on which the childhood development, culminating in the infantile neurosis, is restaged and reactivated in the developmental, crystallization and resolution of the transference neurosis, but as a reflecting mirror, albeit of the unconscious, and characterized by scrupulous neutrality.

This neutrality of the analyst appears to be required by the interests of scientific objectivity, in order to keep the field of observation from being contaminated by the analyst's own emotional intrusions; upon the transference. patient. While the latter position is closely related to the general demand for scientific objectivity and avoidance of the interference of the personal equation. It has its specific relevance for the analytic procedure as such in so far as the analyst is supposed to function not only as an observer of certain processes, but as a mirror which actively reflects back to the patient, the latter's conscious and particularly his unconscious processes through verbal communication. A specific aspect of this neutrality is that the analyst must avoid falling into the role of the environmental figure (or of his opposite). In stead of falling into the assigned role, he must be objectively and neutral enough to reflect back to the patient what roles the latter has assigned to the analyst and to himself in the transference situation. But such objectivity and neutrality now need to be understood more clearly as to their meaning in the therapeutic setting.

To begin. Ego-development is a process of increasingly higher integration and differentiations of the psychic apparatus and does not stop at any given point except in neurosis and psychosis; even though it is true that there is normally a marked consolidation of ego-organization around the period of the Oedipus complex. Another consolidation normally takes place toward the end of adolescence, and further, often less, marked and less visible, consolidation occurs at various other life-stages. These later consolidations—and this is important—follow periods of relative ego-organization and reorganization, characterized by ego-regression. Erikson has described certain types of such periods of ego-regression with subsequent new consolidations as identity crises. An analysis can be characterize, from this standpoint, as a period or periods of induced ego-disorganization and reorganization. Analysis is thus understood as an intervention designed to see the ego-development in motion, be it from a point of relative arrest, or to point of what is conceived of as a healthier direction and/or comprehensiveness of such development this is achieved by the promotion and utilization of (controlled) regression. This regression is one important aspect under which the transference neurosis can be understood, the transference neurosis, in the sense of reactivation of the childhood neurosis, is set in motion not simply by the technical skill of the analyst, but by the fact that the analyst makes between himself available for the development of a new 'object-relationship' between the patient and the analyst. The patient tends to make this potentially new object-relationship into an old one. On the other hand, to the extent to which the patient develops a 'positive transference' (not in the sense of transference as resistance, but in the sense in which 'transference' carries the whole process (of an analysis) he keeps this potentiality of a new object-relationship alive through all the various stages of resistance. The patient can dare to take the plunge into the regressive crises of the transference neurosis which brings him face to face, once, again, with his childhood anxieties and conflicts, of his childhood onto the potentiality of a new object-relationship, represented by the analyst.

We can collectively assume from analytical as well as from life experiences that new spurts of self-development may be intimately connected with such 'regressive' rediscoveries of oneself as may occur through the establishment of new object-relationships, and this means: new discoveries of 'objects.' which to say, that of new discovery of objects and not discovery of new objects, because the essence of such new object-relationships is the opportunity they offer for rediscover y to a new way of relating to objects as well as of being and relating to oneself. This new discovery of oneself and of objects, this reorganization of ego and objects, is made possible by the encounter in order to promote the process. Such a new object-relationship for which the analyst holds himself available to the patient and to which the patient has to hold on throughout the analysis is one meaning of the term 'positive transference.'

What is the neutrality of the analyst? In that of the encounter with a potentially new object, the analyst, which new object has to possess certain qualifications to be able to promote the process of ego-reorganization implicit in the transference neurosis. One of these qualifications is objectivity. This objectivity cannot mean the avoidance of being available to the patient as an object. the objectivity of the analyst has reference to the patient's transference distortions. Increasingly, through the objective analysis of them, the analyst becomes not only potentially but actually available as a new object by eliminating step by step impediments, represented by these transference, to a new object-relationship. There is a tendency to consider the analyst's availability as an object merely as a device on his part to attract transference onto himself. His availability is seen in terms of his being a screen or mirror onto which the patient projects his transference, and which reflects them back to him in the form of interpretations. In this view, the ideal termination point of the analysis no further transference occurs, no projections are thrown on the mirror, the mirror having nothing now to reflect, can be discarded.

This is only a half-truth. The analysis in actuality does not only reflect the transference distorts. In his interpretations he implies aspects of undistorted reality which the patient begins to grasp step by step, as transferences are interpreted. This undistorted realty is mediated to the patient by the analyst, mostly by the process of chiselling away the transference distortions, or, as Freud has beautifully put it, using an expression of Leonardo da Vinci, 'per via di levare' as in sculpturing, not 'per via di porre' as in painting. In sculpturing, the figure to be created comes into being by taking away from the material: In painting, by adding something to the canvas. In analysis, we bring out the true form by taking away the neurotic distortions. However, as in sculpture, we must have, if only in rudiments, an image of that which needs to be brought into its own. The patient, by revealing himself to the analyst provides rudiments of such an on the image through all the distortions—an image which the analyst has to focus in his mind, thus keeping for the patient to whom it is mainly lost. It is this tenuous reciprocal tie which represents the germ of a new object-relationship.

While the relationship between analyst and patient does not possess the structure, scientist—scientific subject, and is not characterized by neutrality in the sense on the part of the analyst, the analyst may become a scientific observer to the extent to which he is able to observe objectivity the patient and himself in interaction. The interaction itself, however, cannot be adequately represented by the model of scientific neutrality. It is unscientifically based on faulty observation, to use this model. The confusion about the issue of countertransference has to do with this. It hardly needs to be pointed out that such a view in no way denies or minimizes the role scientific knowledge, understanding, and methodology play in the analytic process; nor does it have anything to do with advocating an emotionally-charged attitude toward the patient or 'role-taker.' What is to suggest, is to disentangle the justified and necessary requirement of objectivity and neutrality from a model of neutrality which has its origin in propositions which are, as, perhaps, untenable.

One of these is that therapeutic analysis is an objective scientific research method, of a special nature to be sure, but falling within the general category of science as an objective, detached study of natural phenomena, their genesis and interrelations. The ideal image of the analyst is that of a detached scientist. the research method and the investigative procedure in themselves, carried out by this scientist, are said to be therapeutic. It is not self-explanatory why a research project should have a therapeutic effort on the subject of study. The therapeutic effect appears to have something to do with the requirement, in analysis, that the subject, the patient himself, gradually become an associate, as it were, in the research work, that he himself become increasingly engaged in the 'scientific project' which is, of course, directed at himself. We speak of the patient's observing ego on which we need to be able to rely to a certain extent, which we attempt to strengthen and with which we ally ourselves. We encounter and make use of, in other words, what is known under the general title 'identification.' The patient and the analyst identify to an increasing degree, if the analysis proceeds, in their ego-activity of scientifically guided self-scrutiny.

If the possibility and gradual development of such identification is, as is always claimed, a necessary requirement for a successful analysis, this introduces, for then and there a factor which has nothing to do with scientific detachment and the neutrality of a mirror. this identification does have to do with the development of a new object-relationship, in fact, it is the foundation for it.

The transference neurosis takes places in the influential presence of the analyst and, as the analysis progresses, more a nd more 'in the presence" and under the eyes of the patient's observing ego. The scrutiny, carries out t by the analyst and by the patient, is an organizing, 'synthetic' ego-activity. The development of an ego function is dependent on interaction. Neither the self-scrutiny, nor the freer, healthier development of the psychic apparatus whose resumption is contingent upon such scrutiny, take place in the vacuum of scientific laboratory conditions. They take place in the presence of a favourable environment, by interaction with it. One could say that in the analytic process this environmental element, as happens in the original development, becomes increasingly internalized as what we call the observing ego of the patient.

There is another aspect to this peculiarity. Involved in the insistence that the analytic activity is a strictly scientific one (not merely using scientific and methods) is the notion of the dignity of science. scientific man is considered by Freud as the most advanced form of human development. the scientific stage of the development of man's conception of the universe as its counterpart in the individual's state of maturity, according to 'Totem and Taboo.' Scientific self-understanding, to which the patient is helped, is in and by itself therapeutic, following this view, since it implies the movement toward a stage of human evolution of scientific man who understands himself and external reality not in animistic or religious terms but in terms of objective science. There is little doubt that what we call the scientific exploration of the universe, including the self, may lead to greater mastery over it (within certain limits of which we are becoming painfully aware). The activity of mastering it, however, is not itself a scientific activity. If scientific objectivity is assumed to be the mos t mature stage of man's understanding of the universe, indicating the highest degree of the individual's stage of maturity, we ma y have a vested interest in viewing psychoanalytic therapy as a purely scientific activity and its effects as due to such scientific objectivity. beyond the issue. It is believed to be necessary and timely to question the assumption, handed to us from the nineteenth century, that the scientific approach to the world and the self represent a higher and more mature evolutionary stage of man than the religious way of life.

The analyst, through the objective interpretation of transference distortions, increasingly becomes available to the patient as a new object. and this no t primarily in the sense of an object not previously met, but the newness consists in the patient's rediscovery of the early paths of the development of object-relations leading to a new way of relations to objects and of being oneself. Through all the transference distortions the patient reveals rudiments at least of that core (of himself and 'objects') which has been distorted. It is this core, rudimentary and vague as it may be, to which the analyst has reference when he interprets transferences and defences, and not some abstract concept of reality or normality, if he is to reach the patient. If the analyst keeps his central focus on this emerging core he avoids moulding the patient in the analyst's own image or imposing on the patient his own concept of what the patient should become. it requires an objectivity and neutrality the essence of which is love and respect for the individual and for individual development. This love and respect represent the counterpart in 'reality,' and psychic apparatus take place.

The parent-child relationship can serve as a model as for that of the parent ideally is in an empathic relationship of understanding the child's particular stage in development, yet ahead in his vision of the child's future and mediating this vision to the child in his dealing with him. This vision, informed by the parent's own experience and knowledge of growth and future, is, ideally, a more articulate and more integrated version of the core of being which the child presents to the parent. This 'more' that the parent sees and knows, he mediates to the child so that the child in identification with it can grow. The child, by internalizing aspects of the parent, also internalizes the parent's image of bodily of the child—an image which is mediated to the child in the thousand different ways of being handled, bodily and emotionally. Early identification as part of ego-development, built up through introjection of maternal aspects, includes introjection of the mother's image of the child. Part of what is introjected is the image of the child as seen, felt, smelled, heard, touched, by the mother. It would perhaps be more correct to add that what happens is not wholly a process of introjection, If introjection is used as a term for an intrapsychic activity. The bodily handling of and concern with the child, the manner in which the child is fed, touched, cleaned, the way it is looked at, talked and, called by name, recognized and re-recognized—all these and many other ways of communicating with the child, and communicating to him his identity, sameness, unity, and individuality, shape and mould him so that he can begin to identify himself to feel and recognize himself as one and as separate from others yet with others. The child begins to experience himself as a centred unit by being centred upon.

In analysis, if it is to be a process leading to structural changes, interactions of a comparable nature have to take place. At this point, nonetheless, only indicate of these interactions during early development, the positive nature of the neutrality required, which includes the capacity for mature object-relations as manifested in the parent by his or her ability to follow and at the same time be ahead of the child's development.

Mature object-relations are not characterized by a sameness of relatedness but by an optimal range of relatedness and by the ability to relate to different objects according to their particular levels of maturity. In analysis, a mature object-relationship is maintained with a given patient if the analysis relates to the patient in tune with the shifting levels of development manifested by the patient at different times, but always from the viewpoint of potential growth, that is, from the viewpoint of the future. It seems to be the fear of moulding the patient in one's own image which has prevented analysis from coming to grips with the analytic dimension of the future in analytic theory and practice. A strange omission considering the fact that growth and development are at the centre of all psychoanalytic concern. A fresh and deeper approach to the superego problem cannot be taken without facing this issue.

The patient, in order to attain structural changes in his ego-organization, needs the relatedness with a consistently mature object. This, of course, does not mean that during the course of the analysis the analyst is experienced by the patient always or most of the time as a mature object. In the analyst it requires the establishment and exercise of special 'skills' during the analytic hour, similar in structure to other professional skills (including the fact that as a skill it is practised only during the professional work period) and related to the special, but not professionally articulate and concentrate attitudes of parents when dealing with the their children.

Inclining implications do indicate that the activity of the analyst, and specifically his interpretations as well as the ways in which they are integrated by the patient, need to be considered and understood in the terminological psychodymanics of the ego. Such psychodynamics cannot be worked out without proper attention to the functioning of integrative processes in the ego-reality field, beginning with such processes as introjection, identifications, projection (of which we know something), and progressing to their genetic derivatives, modifications, and transformations in later life-stages (of which we understand very little, except in so fa r as they are used for defensive purposes). The more intact the ego of the patient, the more of this integration taking place in the analytic process occurs without being noticed or at least, without being noticed or at least without being considered and conceptualized as an essential element in the analytic process. Classical analysis with classical cases easily leaves unrecognized essential elements of the analytic process, not because they are not present but because they are as difficult to see in such cases as it was difficult to discover 'classical' psychodynamics in normal people. Cases with obvious ego defects magnify what also occurs in the typical analysis of the neuroses, just as in neurotics we see magnified the psychodynamics of human beings in general. This is not to say that there is no difference between the analysis of the classical psychoneuroses and of cases with obvious ego defects, especially in borderline cases and psychoses, processes such as in the child-parent relationship take place in the therapeutic situation on levels relatively close and similar to those of the early child-parent relationship. The further we move away from gross ego defect cases, the more do these integrative processes take place on higher levels of sublimation and by modes of communication which show much more complex stages of organization.

## II

The elaboration assigning the structural point of view in psychoanalytic theory has brought about the danger of isolating the different structures of the psycho apparatus from one another. It may look nowadays as though the ego is a creature of and functioning in conjunction with external reality, whereas the area of the instinctual drives, of the id,. Is as such unrelated to the external world. To use Freud's archeological simile, it is as though the functional relationship between the deeper strata of an excavation and their external environment were denied because these deeper strata are not in a functional relationship with th present-day environment; as though it were maintained that the architectural structures of deeper, earlier strata are due to purely 'internal' processes, in contrast to the functional interrelatedness between present architectural structures (higher, later strata) and the external environment that we see and live in. The id, however—in the archeological analogy being comparable to a deeper, earlier strata—as such integrates with its correlative 'early' external environment as much as the ego integrates with the ego's more 'recent' external reality. The id deals with and is a creature of adaption, just as much as the ego—bu t on a very different level of organization.

The view to the conception of the psychic apparatus as a closed system has a bearing on the traditional notion of the analyst's neutrality and of his function as a mirror. It is in this context as the concept of instinctual drives, and within the particular regards to the relation to objects, as formulated in psychoanalytic theory. In his paper 'Instincts and Their Vicissitudes' Freud's introductory discussion of instincts, he says:

The true beginning of scientific activity consists . . . in describing phenomena and then in proceeding to group, classify and correlate them. Even at the stage of description it is not possible to avoid applying certain abstract ideas to the material in hand, ideas derived from some-where or other but certainly not from the new observations alone. such ideas—which will later become the basic concepts of the science—are still more indispensable as the material is further worked over.'

. . . They must at first necessarily possess some degree of indefiniteness; there can be no question of any clear delimitation of their content. so long as they remain in this condition, we come to an understanding about their meaning by making repeated references to the material of observation from which they appear to have been derived, but upon which, in fact, they have been imposed. Thus, strictly speaking, they are in the nature of conventions—although everything depends on their not being arbitrarily chosen but determined by their having significant relations to the empirical material, relations that we seem to sense before we can clearly recognize and demonstrate them. It is only after more thorough investigation of the field of observation that we are able to formulate its basic scientific concepts with increases precision, and progressively so to modify them that they become serviceable and consistent over a wide area. Then, the time may have come to confine them in definitions. The advance of knowledge, however, does not tolerate any rigidity even in definitions. Physics furnishes an excellent illustration of the way in which even 'basic concepts' that have been established in the form of definitions are constantly being altered in their content. The concept of instinct (Trieb), Freud goes on to say, is such a basic concept, 'conventional but still somewhat obscure,' and thus open to alterations in its content

In the same paper, Freud defines instinct as a stimulus: A stimulus not arising in the outer world but 'from within the organism.' He adds, that 'a better term for an instinctual stimulus is a 'need,' and say's, that such 'stimuli are the signs of an internal world.' Freud lays explicit stress on one fundamental implication of his whole consideration of instincts, namely, that it implies the concept of purpose in the form of what he calls a biological postulate. This postulate runs as follows: The nervous system is an apparatus which has the function of getting rid of the stimuli that reach it, or of reducing them to the lowest possible level.' an instinct is a stimulus from within reaching the nervous system, since an instinct is a stimulus arising within the organism and acting 'always as a constant force, it obliges the nervous system to renounce its ideal intention of keeping off stimuli, and compels it to undertake involved and interconnected activities by which the external world is so changed as to afford satisfaction to the internal source of stimulation.'

Instinct being an inner stimulus reaching the nervous apparatus, the object of an instinct is 'the thing in regard to which or through which the instinct is able to achieve its aim,' this aim being satisfaction. The object of an instinct is further described as 'what is most variable about an instinct 'not ordinally connected with it,' and as becoming 'assigned to it only in consequence of being peculiarly fitted to make satisfaction possible.' It is here that we see instinctual drives being conceived of as 'intrapsychic,' or originally not related to objects.

In his later writings Freud gradually moves away from this position. Instincts are no longer defined as (inner) stimuli with which the nervous apparatus details in accordance with the scheme of the reflex arc, but instinct in '[Beyond the Pleasure Principle] is seen as 'an urge inherent in organic life to restore an earlier state of things which the living entity has been obliged to abandon under the pressure of external disturbing forces. Again, he defines instinct in terms equivalent to the terms he used earlier in describing the function of the nervous apparatus itself, the nervous apparatus, the 'living entity,' in its interchange with 'external disturbing forces.' Instinct is no longer an intrapsychic stimulus, but an expression of the function, the 'urge' of the nervous apparatus to deal with environment. The intimate and fundamental relationship of instinct, especially in so far as libido (sexual instincts, Eros) is concerned, with objects, is more clearly brought out in 'The Problem of Anxiety,' until finally, in his paper, 'An Outline of Psycho-Analysis,' The aim of the first of these basic instincts [Eros] is to establish ever greater unities and to preserve them thus—in short, to bind together. It is noteworthy that not only the relatedness of objects is implicit, the aim of the instinct Eros is no longer formulated in terms of a contentless 'satisfaction,' or satisfaction in the sense of abolishing stimuli, but the aim is clearly seen in terms of integration. It is 'to bind together.' And while Freud feels that it is possible to apply his earlier formula, 'to the effect that instincts tend toward a return to an earlier [inanimate] states,' to the destructive or death instinct, 'we are unable to apply the formula to Eros (the love instinct).'

The basic concept Instinct, has thus changed its content since Freud wrote 'Instincts and Their Vicissitudes.' In his later writings he does not take as his starting point and model the reflex-arc scheme of a self-contained, closed system, but bases his considerations on a much broader, more modern biological framework. And it should be clear from the last inference in mention, that it is by no meas the ego alone to which he assigns the function of synthesis, of binding together. Eros, is one of the two basic instincts, is itself an integrating force. This is in accordance with his concept of primary narcissism as first formulated in 'On Narcissism: an Introduction,' and further elaborate in his later writings, notably in 'Civilization and Its Discontents,' where object, reality, far from being originally not connected with libido, are seen as becoming gradually differentiated from primary narcissistic identity of 'inner; and 'outer' world.

In his conception of Eros, Freud moves away from an opposition between instinctual drives and ego, and toward a view according to which instinctual drives become moulded, channelled, focussed, tamed, transformed and sublimated in or by the ego organization, an organization which is more complex and at the same time, more sharply elaborated and articulate than the drive-organization which we call the id. But the ego is an organization which continues, much more than it is in opposition to, the inherent tendencies of the drive-organization. The concept Eros encompasses in one term one of the two basic tendencies or 'purposes' of the psychic apparatus as manifested on both levels of organization.

In such a perceptive, instinctual drives are as primarily related to 'object,' to the 'external world' as the ego is. The organization of this outer world, of these 'objects' corresponds to the level of drive-organization rather than of ego-organization. In other words, instinctual drives organize environment and are organized by it no less that is true for the ego and its reality. It is the mutuality of organization, in the sense of configuration, each other, which constitutes the inextricable interrelatedness of 'inner and 'outer' world,' It would be justified, as to say of primary and secondary processes not only in reference to the psychic apparatus but also in reference to the outer world in as far as its psychological structure is concerned. The qualitative difference between the two levels of organization might terminologically be indicated by speaking of environment as correlative to drives, and of reality as correlative to ego. Instinctual drives can be seen as originally not connected with objects only in the sense that 'originally' the world is not organized, by primitive psychic apparatus in such a way that objects are differentiated. Out of an 'undifferentiated stage' emerge what have been termed part-object or object-nuclei. A more appropriate term for such pre-stages of an object-world might be the noun 'shapes' in the sense of configurations of an indeterminate degree and a fluidity of organization, and without the connotation of object-fragments.

The preceding excursion into some problems of instinctual-theory is intended to show that the issue of object-relations in psychoanalytic theory has suffered from a formulation of the instinctual-concept according to which instincts, as inner stimuli, are contrasted with outer stimuli, both. Although in different ways, affecting the psychic apparatus. Inner and outer stimuli, terms for inner and outer world on a certain level of abstraction, are thus conceived as originally unrelated or even opposed to each other, but running parallel, as it were, in their relation to the nervous apparatus. And while, Freud in his general trend of though and in many formulations moved away from this framework, psychoanalytic theory remained under it sway except in the realm of ego-psychology, it is unfortunate that the development of ego-psychology had to take place in relative isolation from instinct-theory. It is true that our understanding of instinctual drive has also progressed. But the extremely fruitful concept of organization (the two aspects of which are integrated and differentiated) has been insufficiently, if at all, applied to the understanding of instinctual drives, and instinct-theory has remained under the aegis of the antiquated stimulus-reflex conceptual model—a mechanistic frame of reference far removed from modern psychological as well as biological thought. The scheme of the reflex-arc, as Freud says in 'Instincts and Their Vicissitudes' has been given to us by physiology. But this was the mechanistic physiology of the nineteenth century. Ego-psychology began its development in a quite different climate already, as is clear from Freud's biological reflection in 'Beyond the Pleasure Principle.' Thus, it has come about that the ego is seen as an organ of adaptation to and integration and differentiation with and of the outer world, whereas instinctual drives were left behind in the realm of stimulus-reflex physiology. This, and specifically the conception of instinct as an 'inner' stimulus impinging on the nervous apparatus, has affected the formulations concerning the role of 'objects' in libidinal development and, by extension, has vitiated the understanding of the object-relations between patient and analyst in psychoanalytic treatment.

### III

Returning to the discussion of the analytic situation and the therapeutic process on analysis, it will be useful to dwell further on the dynamics of interaction in early stages of development.

The mother recognizes and fulfills the need of the infant. Both recognition and fulfilment of a need are at firs t beyond the ability of the infant, not merely the fulfilment. The understanding recognition of the infant's need on the part of the mother represents a gathering together of as yet, undifferentiated urges of the infant, urges which in the acts of recognition and fulfilment by the mother undergo a first organization into some directed drive. In a remarkable passage in the 'Project for a Scientific Psychology,' in a chapter which has been called 'The Experience of Satisfaction,' Freud discusses this constellation in its consequences fo r the further organization of the psychic apparatus and in its significance of the need come within the grasp of the growing infant itself. The processes by which this occurs are generally subsumed under the headings identification and introjection. Access to them has to be made available by the environment: the mother, who performs this function in the acts of recognition and fulfilment of the need. These acts are not merely necessary for the physical survival of the infant but necessary at the same time for its psychological development; in so far as they organize, in successive steps, the infant's relatively uncoordinated urges. The whole complex dynamic constellation is one of mutual responsiveness, where nothing is introjected by the infant that is no t brought to it by the mother, although brought by her often unconsciously. and a prerequisite for introjection and identification is gathering mediation of structure and direction by the mother in her caring activities. As the mediating environment conveys structure and direction to the unfolding psychophysical entity, the environment begins to gain structure and direction in the experience of that entity: The environment begins to 'take shape' in the experience of the infant, it is now that identification and introjection as well as projection emerge as more defined processes of organization of the psychic apparatus and of environment.

We arrive at the following formulation: The organization of the psychic apparatus, beyond discernible potentialities at birth (comprising undifferentiated urges and Anlagen of ego-facilities), proceeds by way of mediation of higher organization on the part of the environment to the infantile organism. In one and the same act—as in the same breath and the sucking of milk—drive direction organization of environment into shapes or configurations begin, and they are continued into ego-organization and object-organization, by methods such as identification, introjection, projection. The higher organizational stages of the environment is indispensable for the development of the psychic apparatus and, in early stages, has to be brought to it actively. Without such a 'differential' between organism and environment no development takes place.

The patient, who comes to the analyst for help through increased self-understanding, is led to this self-understanding by the understanding. Whether he verbalizes his understanding to the patient on the level of clarifications of conscious material, whether he indicates or reiterates his intent of understanding, restates the procedure to be followed, or whether he interprets unconscious, verbal or other, material, and especially if he interprets transference and resistance—the analyst structures and articulates, or works toward structuring and articulating the material and the production offered by the patient. If an interpretation of unconscious meaning is timely, the words by which this meaning is expressed are recognized to the patient as expressions of what he experiences. They organize for him what was previously less organized and thus give him a 'distance' from himself which enable him to understand, to see, to put into words and to 'handle' what was previously not visible, understandable, speakable, tangible. A higher stage of organization, of both himself and his environment is thus reached, by way of the organizing understanding which the analyst provides. The analyst functions as a representatives organization and mediate to what is, and the way in which it is, in need of organization.

Nonetheless, of these integrative experiences in analysis are those of the experiences of interaction, comparable in their structure and significance to the early understanding between mother and child. The latter is a model, and as such always of limited value, but a model whose usefulness has recently been stressed by a number of analysts, i.e., René Spitz, and which in its full implication and in its perceptive is a radical departure from the classical 'mirror model.'

Interaction in analysis takes place on much higher level of organization. Communication is carried on predominantly by way of the linguistics of a language, an instrument of and for secondary processes. The satisfaction involve in the analytic interaction is a sublimated one, in increasing degree as the analysis progresses. Satisfaction now has to be understood, not in terms of abolition or reduction of stimulation leading back to a previous state of equilibrium, but in terms of absorbing and integrating 'stimuli,' leading to higher levels of equilibrium. This, it is true, is often achieved by temporary regression to an earlier level, but this regression is 'in the service of the ego,' that is, in the service of higher organization. Satisfaction, in the creation of an identity of experience in two 'systems,' two psychic apparatuses of different levels of organization, thus, containing the potential of growth. This identity is achieved by overcoming a differential. Properly speaking, where there is no experience of satisfaction and no integrative experience where there is no differential to be overcome, where identity is 'given,' that is existing rather than to be created by interaction. An approximate model of such existing identity is perhaps, of providing the intra-uterine situation, and decreasingly in early months of life in the symbiotic relationship of mother and infant.

Analytic interpretations present, on higher levels of interaction, the mutual recognition involved in the creation of identity of experience in two individuals of different levels of ego-organization. Insight gained in such interaction is an integrative experience. The interpretation represents the recognition and understanding which makes available to the patient, means lifting it to the level of the preconscious system, of secondary processes, by the operation of certain types of secondary processes on the part of the analyst. Material organized on or close to the level of drive-organization, of the primary process, and isolated from the preconscious system, is made available for organization on the level of the preconscious system by the analyst's interpretation: A secondary process operation which mediates to the patient secondary process organization. Whether this mediation is successful or not depends, among other things, on the organizing strength of the patient's ego attained through earlier steps in ego-integration, in previous phases of the analysis, and ultimately in his earlier life. To the extent to which such strength is lacking, analysis—organizing interaction by way of linguistic languages communication—becomes less feasible.

An interpretation can be said to comprise two elements, inseparable from each other. The interpretation takes with the patient the step toward true regression, as against the neurotic compromise formation, thus clarifying for the patient his true regression-level which has been covered and made unrecognizable by defensive operations and structures. Secondly, by this very step it mediates to the patient the higher integrative level to be reached. The interpretation thus creates the possibility for freer interplay between the unconscious and preconscious systems, whereby the preconscious regains its originality and intensity, lost to the unconscious in the repression, and the unconscious regains access to land capacity for progression in the direction of higher organization. Put in terms of Freud's metapsychological language. The barrier between unconscious and preconscious, consisting of the archaic cathexis (repetition compulsion) of the unconscious and warding-off anticathexis of the preconscious, is temporarily overcome. This process may be seen as the internalized version of the overcoming of a differential in the interaction process described as integrative experience. Internalization itself is dependent on interaction and is made possible again in the analytic process. The analytic process then consist s in certain integrative analyst as the experiences between patient and analyst as the foundation for the internalized version of such experiences: reorganization of ego, 'structural change.'

The analyst in his interpretation reorganizes, reintegrates unconscious material for himself as well as for the patient, since he has to be attuned to the patient's unconscious, using as we say, his own unconscious as a tool, in order to arrive at the organizing interpretation. The analyst has to move freely between the unconscious and the organization of it in thought and language, for and with the patient. If this is not so—a good example is most instances of the use of technical language—language is used as a defence against leading the unconscious material into ego-organization, and ego-activity as a defence against integration. It is the weakness of the 'strong' ego—strong is its defences—that it guides the psychic apparatus into excluding the unconscious (for instance, by repression or isolation) rather than into lifting the unconscious to a higher organization and, at the same time, holding it available for replenishing regression to it.

Language, when not defensively oriented to be employed by the patient for communication which attempts to reach the analyst on his presumed or actual level of maturity in order to achieve the integrative experience longed for. The analytic patient, while striving for improvement in terms of inner reorganization, is constantly tempted to seek improvement in terms of unsubliminated satisfaction through interaction with the analyst on levels closer to the primary process, rather than in terms of internalization of integrative experience. As is achieved in the process which Freud has described as: Where there was id there shall be ego. The analyst, in his communication through language, mediates higher organization of material hitherto less highly organized, to the patient. This can occur only if two conditions are fulfilled: (a) the patient, through a sufficiently strong 'positive transference' to the analyst, becomes again available for integrative work with himself and his world, as against defensive warding-off of psychic and external reality manifested in the analytic situation in resistance. (b) The analyst must be in time with the patient's productions, that is, he must be able to regress within himself to the level of organization on which the patient is stuck, and to help the patient, by the analysis of defence and resistance, to realize this regression. This realization is prevented by the compromise formations of the neurosis and is made possible by dissolving them into the components of a subjugated unconscious and a superimposed preconscious. By an interpretation, both the unconscious experience and a higher organizational level of that experience are made available to the patient: unconscious and preconscious are joined together in the act of interpretation. In a well-going analysis the patient increasingly becomes enabled to perform this joining himself.

Ordinarily we operate with material organized on high levels of sublimation as 'given reality.' In an analysis the analyst has to retrace the organizational steps which have led to such a reality-level so that the organizing process becomes available to the patient. This is regression in the service of the ego, in the service of reorganization—a regression against which there is resistance in the analyst as well as in the patient. As an often necessary defence against the relatively unorganized power of the unconscious, we tend to automatize higher organizational levels and resist regression out of fear, least we may not find the way back to higher organization. The fear of reliving the past in fear or toppling off a plateau we have reached, and fear of that more chaotic past itself, not only in the sense of past content but more essentially of past, less stable of organization of experience, whose genuine reintegration requires psychic 'work.' Related to it is the fear of the future, pregnant with new integrative tasks and the risk of losing what had been secured. In analysis such fear of the future may be manifested in the patient's defensive clinging to regressed, but seemingly safe levels.

Once the patient is able to speak, nondefensively, from the true level of regression which he has been helped to reach by analysis of defences, he himself, by putting his experience into words, begins to use language creatively, that is, begins to create insight. The patient, by speaking to the analyst attempts to reach the analyst as a representative of higher stages of ego-reality organization, and thus may be said to create insight for himself in the process of language-communications with the analyst as such a representative. such communication on the part of the patient is possible if the analyst, by way of his communisations, in revealing himself to the patient as a more mature person, as a person who can feel with the patient, what the patient experiences and how he experiences it, and who understands it as something more than it has been for the patient. It is this something more, not necessarily more in content but more in organization and significance, that 'external reality' represented and mediated by the analyst, has to offer to the individual and for which the individual is striving. The analyst is doing his part of the work, experiences the cathartic effect of 'regression in the service of he ego' and perform a piece of self-analysis or re-analysis. Freud has remarked that his own self-analysis proceeded by way of analysing patients, and that this was necessary in order to gain the psychic distance required for any such work.

The patient, being recognized by the analyst as something more than he is at present, can attempt to reach this something, more by his communisations to the analyst which may establish a new identity with reality. To varying degrees patients are striving for this integrative experience, though and despite their resistance. To varying degrees patients have given up this striving above the level of omnipotent, magical identification, and to that extent are less available for the analytic process. The therapist, depending on the mobility and potential strength of integrative mechanisms in the patient, has to be more or less explicit and 'primitive' in his ways of communicating to the patients availability as a mature object and his own integrative processes. As this can be called as for the analysis of organizing, restructuring interaction between patient and therapist, which is predominantly performed on the level of language communication. It is likely that the development of language communication. It is likely that the development with 'objects,' is related to the child's reaching, at least in a first approximation, the oedipal stage of psychosexual development, the inner connexions between the development of language, the formation of ego and of objects, and the oedipal phase of psychosexual development, are still to be explored. If such connexions exist, such that they are, then it is not mere arbitrariness to distinguish analysis proper from more primitive means of integrative interaction. To set up rigid boundary lines, however, is to ignore or deny the complexities of the development and of the dynamics of the psychic apparatus.

## IV

In this part of the therapeutic action of psychoanalysis is to further by reexamining certain aspects of the concept and the phenomenon of transference. In contrast to trends in modern psychoanalytic thought to narrow the term transference down to a very specific limited meaning, as will be made to regain th original richness of interrelated phenomena and mental mechanisms which the concept encompasses, and to contribute to the clarification of such interrelations. When Freud speaks of transference neuroses in contradistinction to narcissistic neuroses, two meanings of the term transference are invoked: (a) the transference of libido, contained in the 'ego,' to objects, in the transference neuroses, while in the narcissistic neuroses the libido remains in or is taken back into the 'ego' not 'transferred' to objects. Transference in this sense is virtually synonymous with object-cathexis. To quote from an important early paper on transference: 'The first loving and hating is a transference of auto-erotic pleasant and unpleasant feelings on the objects that evoke these feelings. The first 'object-love' and the first 'object-hate' are, so to speak, the primordial transference . . .' (ii) The second meaning of transference, when distinguishing transference neuroses from narcissistic neuroses, is that of transfer of relations with infantile objects on to objects, and especially to the analyst in the analytic situation.

The second meaning of the term is today the one most frequently referred to, to the exclusion of other meanings. Two recent representative papers on the subject of transference, as Waelder, in his Geneva Congress paper, 'Introduction to the Discussion on Problems of Transference.' saying that: 'Transference may be said to be an attempt of the patient to revive and re-enact, in the analytic situation and in relation to the analyst, situations and fantasies of his childhood.' As well, Hoffer, in his paper, presented at the same Congress, on 'Transference and Transference Neurosis' states: 'The term 'transference' refers to the generally agreed fact that people when entering into any form of object-relationship . . . , transfer upon their objects those images which they encountered in the course of previous infantile experiences . . . . The term 'transference' stresses an aspect of the influence our childhood has on our life as a whole, thus refers to those observations in which people in their contacts with objects, which may be real in imaginary, positive, negative, or ambivalent, 'transfer' their memories of significant previous experiences, and thus 'change the reality' of their objects, invest them with qualities from the past . . . .

The transference neuroses, thus, are characterized by the transfer of libido to external objects as against the attachment of the libido to the 'ego' in the narcissistic affections, and., secondly, by the transfer of libidinal cathexes (and defences against them), originally related to infantile objects, on to contemporary objects.

Transference neuroses as distinguished from narcissistic neurosis is a nosological designation with the term. At the same time, the term 'transference neurosis' is used in a technical sense to designate the revival of the infantile neurosis in the analytic situation. In this sense of the term, the accent is on the second meaning of transference, since the revival of the infantile neurosis is due to the transfer of relations with infantile objects on the contemporary object, the analyst. It is, however, only on the basis of transfer of libido to (external) objects in childhood that libidinal attachments to infantile objects can be transferred to contemporary objects. The first meaning of transference, therefore, is implicit in the technical concept of transference neurosis.

The narcissistic neuroses were thought to be inaccessible to psychoanalytic treatment because of the narcissistic libido cathexis. Psychoanalysis was considered to be feasible only where a 'transference relationship' with the analyst could be established; in the group of disorders, in other words, where emotional development had taken place to the point that transfer of libido to external objects had occurred to a significant degree. If today we consider schizophrenics capable of transference, we hold that they do relate in some way to objects, i.e., to pre-stages of objects which are less 'objective' than oedipal objects narcissistic and object libido, ego and objects are not yet clearly differentiated; this implies the concept of primary narcissism in its full sense. And we hold (ii) that schizophrenics transfer this early type of relatedness onto contemporary 'objects,' which objects thus become less objective, if ego and objects are not clearly differentiated, if ego boundaries and object boundaries are not clearly established, the character of transference also is different, in as much as ego and objects are still largely merged; objects—'different objects'—are not yet clearly differentiated one from the other, and especially not early from contemporary ones. The transference is a much more primitive and 'massive' period. It has been questioned whether one can speak of transference in the sense in which adult neurotic patients manifest it. The conception of such a primitive form of transference is fundamentally different from the assumption of an unrelatedness of ego and objects as is implied in the idea of a withdrawal of libido from objects into the ego.

The modification of our view on the narcissistic affections in this respect, based on clinical experience with schizophrenics and on deepened understandings of early ego-development, leads to a broadened conception of transference in the first-mentioned meaning of that term. To be more precise: Transference, in the sense of transfer of libido to objects in clarified genetically, it develops out of a primary lack of differentiation of ego and objects and thus may regress, as in schizophrenia, to such a pre-stage. Transference does not disappear in the narcissistic affections, by 'withdrawal of libido cathexes into the ego'; it is undifferentiated in a regressive direction toward its origins in the ego-object identity of primary narcissism.

An apparently quite unrelated meaning of transference is found in Freud's paper on 'The Interpretation of Dreams,' in the context of a discussion of the importance of day residues in dreams. Nonetheless, this last meaning of transference to be fundamental for a deeper understanding of the phenomenon of transference, which is to say, 'we learn from [the psychology of the neuroses] that an unconscious idea is as such quite incapable of entering the preconscious and that it can only exercise any effect there by establishing a connection with an idea which already belongs to the preconscious, by transferring its intensity on to it and by getting itself 'covered' by it, least of mention, we have the fact of 'transference' which provides an explanation of so many striking phenomena in the mental life of neurotics. The preconscious idea, which thus acquires an undeserved degree of intensity, may either be left unaltered by the transference, or it may have a modification forced upon it, derived from the content of the idea which effects the transference. And later, again referring to day residues . . . the fact recent elements occur with such regularity points to the existence of a need fo r transference,' 'It will be seen, then, that the day's residues . . . not only borrow something from the unconscious when they succeed in taking a share in the formation of the dream—namely, the instinctual force which is at the disposal of the repressed wish—but that they also offer the unconscious something indispensable—namely the necessary point of attachment for a transference. If we wished to penetrate more deeply at this point into the processes of the mind, we should have to throw more light upon the interplay of excitations between the preconscious and the unconscious—its subject toward which the study of the psychoneuroses draw us, but upon which, as it happens, dreams have no help to offer.'

One parallel between this meaning of transference and the one already mentioned above (ii)—transfer of infantile object-cathexes to contemporary objects—emerges: The unconscious idea, transferring its intensity to a preconscious idea and getting itself 'covered' by it, corresponding to the infantile object-cathexis, whereas the preconscious idea corresponds to the contemporary object-relationship to which the infantile object-cathexis is transferred.

Transference is described in detail by Freud in the chapter on psychotherapy in 'Studies on Hysteria.' It is seen there as due to the mechanism of 'false' (wrong) connection. Freud discusses this mechanism in 'Studies on Hysteria' were he refers to a 'compulsion to associate' the unconscious complex with one that is conscious and reminds us that the mechanism of compulsive ideas in compulsion neurosis is of a similar nature. Also, in the paper 'The Defence Neuro-Psychoses' the 'false connection' of course, is also involved in the explanation of screen memories, where it is called 'displacement.' The German term for screen memories, 'Deck-Erinnerungen,' uses the sam e word 'decken,' to cover, which is used from 'The Interpretation of Dreams' where the unconscious idea gets itself 'covered' by the preconscious idea.

While these mechanisms involved in the 'interplay of excitations between the preconscious and the unconscious' have reference to the psychoneuroses and the dream and were discovered and described in those contexts, they are only the more or less pathological, magnified or distorted versions of normal mechanisms. Similarly the transfer of libido to objects and the transfer of infantile object-relations to contemporary ones are normal processes, seen in neurosis in pathological modifications and distortions.

The compulsion to associate the unconscious complex with one that is conscious is the same phenomenon as the need for transference in the quotation from 'The Interpretation of Dreams,' as having to do with the indestructibility of all mental acts which are truly unconscious. This indestructibility of unconscious mental acts is compared by Freud to the ghost s in the underworld of the Odyssey,' 'ghosts which awoke to new life as soon as they tasted blood, the blood of conscious-preconscious life, the life of 'contemporary' present-day objects. It is a short step from here to the view of transference as a manifestation of the repetition compulsion.

The transference neurosis, in the technical sense of the establishment and resolution of it in the analytic process, is due to the blood of recognition which the patient's unconscious is given to taste—so that the old ghosts may re-awaken to life. Those who know ghosts tell us that they long to be released from their ghost-life and led to rest as ancestors. As ancestors they live forth in the present generation, while as ghosts they are compelled to haunt the present generation with their shadow-life. Transference is pathological in so far as the unconscious is a crowd of ghosts, and this is the beginning of the transference neurosis in analysis: Ghosts of the unconscious, imprisoned by defences but haunting the patient in the dark of his daylight of analysis the ghosts of the unconscious are laid and led to rest as ancestors whose power is taken over and transformed into the newer intensity of present life, of the secondary process and contemporary objects.

In the development of the psychic apparatus the secondary process, preconscious organization, is the manifestation and result of interaction between a more primitively organized psychic apparatus and the secondary process activity of the environment; through such interaction the unconscious gains higher organization. Such ego-development helps to revive the repressed unconscious of the patient by his recognition of it. Through interpretation of transference and resistance, through the recovery of memories and through reconstruction, the patient's unconscious activity is led into preconscious organization. The analyst, in the analytic situation, offers himself to the patient as a contemporary object. As such he revives the ghosts of the unconscious for the patient by fostering the transference neurosis which comes about in the same way in which the dream comes about. Through the mutual attraction of unconscious and 'recent' day residue elements, dream interpretation and interpretation of transference have this function in common; they both attempt to re-establish the lost connexion, the buried interplay, between the unconscious and the preconscious.

Transferences studied in neurosis and analysed in therapeutic analysis are the diseased manifestations of the life of that indestructible unconscious whose 'attachments' to 'recent elements,' by way of transformation of primary into secondary processes, constitute growth. There is no greater misunderstanding of the full meaning of transference than the one most clearly expressed in a formulation by Silverberg, but shared by many analysts. Silverberg, in his paper on 'The Concept of Transference,' writes: 'The wide prevalence of the dynamism of transference among human beings is a mark of man's immaturity, and it may be expected in ages to come that, as man progressively matures . . . transference will gradually vanish from his psychic repertory. But far from being, as Silverberg puts it, 'the enduring monument of man's profound rebellion against reality and his stubborn persistence in the ways of immaturity, transference is the 'dynamism' by which the instinctual life of man, the id, becomes ego and by which reality becomes integrated and maturity is achieved. Without such transference—of the intensity of the unconscious, of the infantile ways of experiencing life which has no language and little organization, but the indestructibility and power of the origins of life—to preconscious and to present-day life and contemporary objects—without such transference, or to the extent to which such transference, miscarries, human life becomes sterile and an empty shell. On the other hand, the unconscious needs present-day external reality (objects) and present-day psychic reality (the preconscious) for its own continuity, least it be condemned to life the shadow-life of ghosts or to destroy life.

In the development of preconscious mental organization—and this is resumed in the analytic process—transformation of primary into secondary process activity is contingent upon a differential, a (libidinal) tension-system between primary and secondary process organization, that is, between the infantile organism, its psychic apparatus, and the more structured environment; transference in the sense of an evolving relationship with 'objects.' This interaction is the basis for the so-called 'integrative experience.' The relationship is a mutual one—as is the interplay of excitations between unconscious and preconscious—since the environment not only has to make itself available and move in a regressive direction toward the more primitively organized psychic apparatus; the environment also needs the latter as an external representative of its own unconscious levels of organization with which communication is to be maintained. The analytic process, in the development and resolution of the transference neurosis, is a repetition—with essential modifications because taking place on another level—of such a libidinal tension-system between a more primitively and a more maturely organized psychic apparatus.

The differential, implicit in the integrative experience, we meet again, internalized, in the form of the tension-system constituting the interplay of excitations between the preconscious and the unconscious. We postulate thus internalization of an interaction-process, not simply internalization of 'objects,' as an essential element in ego-development as well as in the resumption of it in analysis. The double aspect of transference, the fact that transference refers to the interaction between psychic apparatus and object-world as well as the interplay between the unconscious and the preconscious, within the psychic apparatus thus becomes clarified. The opening up of barriers between unconscious and preconscious, as it occurs in any creative process, is then to be understood as an internalized integrative experience—and is in fact experienced as such.

The intensity of unconscious processes and experiences is transferred to preconscious experiences. Our present, current experience have intensity and depth to the extent to which they are in communication (interplay) with the unconscious, infantile, experiences representing the indestructible matrix of all subsequent experiences. Freud, in 1897, was well aware of this. In a letter to Fliess he writes, after recounting experiences with his younger brother and his nephew between the ages of 1 and 2 years: 'My nephew and younger brother determined, not only the neurotic side of all my friendships, but also their depth.'

The unconscious suffers under repression because its need for transference is inhibited. It finds an outlet in neurotic transference, 'repetitions' which fail to achieve higher integration ('wrong connections'). The preconscious suffers no less from repression since it has no access to the unconscious intensities, the unconscious prototypical experiences which give current experiences their full meaning and emotional depth. In promoting the transference neurosis, we are promoting a regressive movement on the part of the preconscious (ego-regression) which is designed to bring the preconscious out of its defensive isolation from the unconscious and to allow the unconscious to re-cathect, in interaction with the analyst, preconscious ideas and experiences in such a way that higher organization of mental life can come about. The mediator of this interplay of transference is the analyst who, as a necessary point of attachment for a transference. As a contemporary object, the analyst represents a psychic apparatus whose secondary process organization is stable and capable of controlled regression so that he is optimally in communication with both his own and the patient's unconscious, so as to serve as a reliable mediator and partner of communication, of transference between unconscious and preconscious, and thus of higher, interpretational organization of both.

The integration of ego and reality consists, and the continued integrity of ego and reality depends on, transference of unconscious processes and 'contents' onto new experiences and objects of contemporary life. in pathological transference the transformation of primary into secondary processes and the continued interplay between them has been replaced by super-impositions of secondary on primary processes, so that they exist side by side, isolated from each other. Freud has described this constellation in his paper on 'The Unconscious.' Actually there is no lifting of the repression until the conscious idea, after the resistances have been overcome has entered into connection with the unconscious memory-trace. it is only through the making conscious of the latter 'the identity of the information given to the patient by with his repressed memory is only apparent. To have heard something and to have experienced something are in their psychological nature two different things, even though the content of both is the same and later, in the same paper, Freud speaks of the thing-cathexes of objects in the unconscious, whereas the 'conscious presentation comprises the presentation of the thing [thing cathexis] plus the presentation of the word belonging to it. And further: 'The systems preconscious comes about by this thing-presentation being hypercathected through being linked with the word-presentation corresponding to it. These hypercathexes, we may suppose, that brings about a higher psychical succeeded by secondary process which is primary process to be succeeded by the secondary process which is dominant in the preconscious. Now, too, we are in a position to state precisely what it is that repression denies to both the rejected presentation in the transference neuroses: what it denies to the rejected presentation in the transference neurosis; what it denies to the presentation is yo the presentation is the translation into words which shall remain attached to the object.

The correspondence of verbal ideas to concrete ideas, that is to things-cathexes in the unconscious, is mediated to the developing infantile psychic apparatus by the adult environment. The hypercathexes which 'bring about a higher psychical organization,' consisting in a linking up of unconscious memory traces with verbal ideas corresponding to them, are, in early ego-development, due to the organizing interaction between primary processes activity of the child's environment. The terms 'differential' and 'libidinal tension-system' as designated in the energy-aspects of this interaction, sources of energy of such hypercathexes. Freud clearly approached the problem of interaction between psychic apparatuses of different levels of organization when he spoke of the linking of concrete ideas in the unconscious with verbal ideas as constituting the hypercathexes which 'bring about a higher psychical organization.' For this 'linking up' is the same phenomenon as the mediation of higher organization, of preconscious mental activity, on the part of the child's environment, to the infantile psychic apparatus. Verbal ideas are representatives of preconscious activity, representatives of special importance because of the special role language plays in the higher development of the psychic apparatus, but they are, of course, not the only ones. Such linking up occurring in the interaction process becomes increasingly internalized as the interplay and communication between unconscious and preconscious within the psychic apparatus. The need for resumption of such mediating interact in analysis, so that new internalisation may become possible and internal interaction be reactivated, results from the pathological degree of isolation between unconscious and preconscious, or—to speak in terms of a later terminology—from the development of defence processes of such proportions that the ego, rather than maintaining or extending its organization of the realm of the unconscious, excludes more and more from its reach.

Incidently, the view of transference which stresses the need of the unconscious for transference, for a point of attachment for a transference in the preconscious, by which primary process is transformed into secondary process—implies the notion that psychic health has to do with an optimal, although by no means necessarily conscious, communication between unconscious and preconscious, between the infantile, archaic stages and structures of the psychic apparatus and its later stages as structures of organization. And further, that the unconscious is capable of change and, as Freud say s, 'accessible to the impression of life, and of the preconscious. Where repression is lifted and unconscious and preconscious are again, in communication, infantile object and contemporary object ma y be united into one—a truly new object as both unconscious and preconscious are changed by their mutual communication. The object which helps to bring this about in therapy, the analyst, mediates this union—a new version of the way in which transformation of primary into secondary processes opened up in childhood, through mediation of higher organization by way of early object-relations.

A few words about transference and the so-called 'real relationship' between patient and analyst, it has been said that one should distinguish transference (and countertransference) between patient and analyst in the analytic situation from the 'realistic' relationship between the two. However, it is implied in such statements that the realistic relationship between patient and analyst has nothing to do with transference, least of mention, that there is neither such a thing as reality nor a real relationship, without transference any 'real relationship' involves transfer of unconscious imagines to present-day objects. In fact, present-day objects are objects, and thus 'real,' in the full sense of the word (which comprises the unity of unconscious memory traces and preconscious idea) only to the extent to which this transference, in the sense of transformational interplay between unconscious and preconscious, is realized. The 'resolution of the transference' at the termination of analysis means resolution of the transference neurosis, and thereby of the transference distortions. This includes the recognition of the limited nature of any human relationship and of the specific limitations of the patient-analyst relationship. But the new object-relationship with the analyst, which is gradually being built in the course of the analysis and constitutes the real relationship between patient and analyst, and which serves as a focal point for the establishment of healthier object-relations in the patient's 'real' life, is not devoid of transference in the sense that has been clarified.

. . . To the extent to which the patient develops a 'positive transference' (not in the sense of transference as resistance, but in the sense of that 'transference' which carries the whole process of analysis) he keeps this potentiality of a new object-relationship alive through all the various stages of resistance. The meaning of positive transference tends to be discredited in modern analytic writing and teaching, although not in treatment itself

Freud, like any man who does not sacrifice the plexuities of life to the deceptive simplicity of rigid concepts, has said a good many contradictory things. He can be quoted in support of many different ideas.

He writes to Jung on 6 December, 1906: 'It would not have escaped you that our cures come about through attaching the libido reigning in the subconscious (transference) . . . Where this fails the patient will not make the effort or else does not listen when we translate his material to him. It is in essence a cure through love. Moreover, it is transference that provides the strongest proof, the only unassailable one, for the relationship of neuroses to love.' And he writes to Ferenczi, on 10 January, 1910: 'I will present you with some theory that has occurred to me while reading your analysis [referring to Ferenczi's self analysis of a dream]. It seems to m e that in our influencing of the sexual impulse we cannot achieve anything other than exchanges and displacements, never renunciation, relinquishment or the resolution of a complex. When someone brings out his infantile plexuities he has saved part of them (the effect) in a current form (transference). He has shed a skin and leaves it for the analyst. God forbid that he should now be naked, without a skin.

# REFERENCES

- Ferenczi, S. Introjection and Transference. In: Sex in Psychoanalysis, p. 49 (New York: Brunner, 1950.)
- Fisher, Charles (1956). Dreams, Images and Perception. J. Amer. Psa. Assn., 4.
- Freud, S. Instincts and Their Vicissitudes. S.E., 14.
  -Beyond the Pleasure Principle. S. E., 18.
  -An Outline of Psycho-analysis. S.E., 18.
  -The Origins of Psychoanalysis. (London: Hogarth, 1940).
  -The Interpretation of Dreams. S.E. 5.
  -Studies on Hysteria. S.E. 2.
  -The Defence Neur.-Psychoses, Collected Papers. I. 66.
  -Screen Memories, Collected Papers. 5, 52.
  -The Unconscious. S.E. 14.
- Hoffer, W. Transference and Transference Neurosis. Int. J. Psycho-Anal., 37. 377.
- Jones, E. The Life and Work of Sigmund Freud, Vol.2 (London: Hogarth, 1955.)
- Loewald, H.W. (1951): Ego and Reality, In: T. J. Psycho-Anal., 32.
- Rycroft, C. The Nature and Function of the Analysts Communication to the Patient. Int. J. Pyscho-Anal., 37. 470.
- Silverberg. W. The Concept of Transference. Psa. Assn. 4.
- Spitz, R. (1956). Countertransference. J. Amer. Psa. Assn., 4.
- Tower, L. (1956): Countertransference. J. Amer. Psa. Assn., 4
- Waelder, R. Introduction to the Discussion on Problems of Transference, Int. J. Psycho-Anal., 37, 367.

Lightning Source UK Ltd.
Milton Keynes UK
UKOW03f2059281116

288751UK00001B/216/P